CROSSING]
AROUND ᴮᴿᴵˢᵀᴼᴸ
OFF-ROAD ON FOOT
2: Beyond the Urban Fringe

Christopher Bloor

Closer to the Countryside

First published in 2008 by
Closer to the Countryside (Books)
161, Wellington Hill West,
Henleaze,
Bristol BS9 4QW
www.closertothecountryside.co.uk

ISBN 978-0-9555461-1-2

Cover photograph Dylan Arnold ©
Typesetting and cover design Sally Mundy

Printed in the UK by Cpod, Trowbridge, Wiltshire

CONTENTS

INTRODUCTION

This second book of walks around Bristol, explores the countryside beyond the Community Forest Path encircling the city. It builds on the ground established in the first book in the series, **Out from the Centre**, which had at its heart the thought that inspired the Community Forest Path, namely the idea of leading people out into the countryside. There are two reasons why this is a positive thing to do: firstly, it provides an easily accessible form of exercise and secondly, it provides an intimate yet uncompromising view of the landscape.

Any one who wears spectacles will be particularly aware that nearly all of us spend most of our time looking at the world through glass – the windows of houses and offices, windscreens, television screens and computer monitors – some people even believe that they have not really seen a site until it has been captured by a camera. So, when we begin to explore the paths around our homes without these obstructions, we become aware of a different order of reality. We can feel the sun and breezes on our faces – but also rain and sleet. We can sense grass, mud and stones under our feet – but also nettles on our legs and the tug of brambles on our sleeves. We can hear birdsong and the sound of the wind in the trees – but also, on occasion, the threatening growl of an undisciplined dog. We can smell roses and ramsons and the scent of rosemary on our fingers – but sometimes the sour smell of sulphur seeping out of landfill sites.

These multi-sensory adventures reflect the fact that the world of footpaths is unedited by any deliberate hand. Those which survive are the accidental leavings of other ages – some linking living-spaces to work-places – often long since abandoned – and more connecting parishioners to places of worship, which rarely ring with the lusty singing of former congregations. Thus the exploration of a footpath is often a trip into the past – an archaeological journey across a fossil landscape, where the green fingers of an older reality still linger. However, this is not an exercise in nostalgia. The paths explored cut across noisy, much-frequented thoroughfares and open up alternative perspectives, which allow us look at things against the grain of the planned urban landscape.

As we step **Beyond the Urban Fringe** the nature of the landscape changes. Whereas, in **'Out from the Centre'**, most of the routes might be described as off-road routes in an urban or suburban setting, only lightly touched by modern agriculture; most of the routes in this book go through working farmland, thus establishing contact with the modern essence of the countryside. Here we see wheeling buzzards and grazing sheep (occasionally stuck in sheep netting or brambles.) and may be alarmed by curious cattle and horses. One moment, we are picking our way across arable land and the next we are enjoying the resilience of meadow grass under our feet and the chuckle of running water at the field-edge, until we come across the resultant mud in the next gateway.

But to actually step across the boundary between urban and rural is not without difficulties, mainly because the suburbs have been imposed on the rural landscape in a manner that a geologist might call "unconformable". The houses have been planned to relate to the road network that links them to the city and not to the surrounding countryside. This creates an artificial disjunction between the town and the countryside on which it ultimately depends.

This split has been reinforced by municipal negligence, which came to my notice as I was researching these books. For example, I had to abandon one route from Whitchurch leisure centre, because the council had allowed the right of way up to Maes Knoll to lapse over a thirty metre stretch on the edge of the estate. The route down the Dundry Slopes to Hartcliffe in **Out from the Centre** is also problematic because a section of publicly owned land becomes unpleasantly overgrown with nettles and brambles in summer. The second route in this book also comes with a health warning for the same reason.

This planned and reinforced division between town and country has unfortunate consequences, as can be seen, for example, along East Dundry Lane, which is treated as a tip by the jobbing builders of the estates below. This is not a class issue, because from Stoke Bishop to Lawrence Weston and from Westbury on Trym to Filwood Park, individuals tip rubbish onto public paths at the bottom of their gardens wherever they do not feel a connection with the unseen space beyond.

One of the main aims of this series is to promote conversations across the rural-urban boundary. This is the reason why I have included so many pubs. In many places, the local pub is the only place that gives reality to a community, which would otherwise be merely a collection of houses. Any community forest walk should include a visit to a pub, where you are bound to enter into dialogue with members of the local community, unless you are stuck within the confines of a group of your own. You can always order a soft drink or a cup of coffee if you are not a beer drinker like me.

As a runner, I prefer to drink after I have completed a route, because running with a belly full of beer is neither comfortable nor advisable. But I am also a walker, and when I walk, I prefer to have a drink half way round. Thus, all but two of the routes offer opportunities for a half way pit-stop and some of them would make strenuous pub crawls. (The importance of pubs has been emphasised in this book by the addition of black and white photographs, which punctuate the text in much the same way as a pub stop punctuates a walk in the country.)

If the physical experience of using footpaths around the edge of the city raises questions about the relationship between town and country, the intellectual experience of trying to write about them challenges one to find answers within an overarching philosophy. I have always been aware of a connection between the countryside and spirituality, which, in these islands, can be traced back at least as far as the writings of the early Celtic church. And even the most secular minded people have felt that a connection with the countryside has spiritual – or psychological – benefits – (the terms have similar origins). Walking in the open air with ones feet in the mud confers a 'grounded-ness' that is spiritual as well as literal. But in the process of producing this book, vague spirituality has developed a particular form.

The starting point for this development was the set of figurative maps, which is a unique feature of the series. The maps came about through a mixture of imagination and cartographic incompetence, when it became apparent that some sort of diagram was necessary for each route. The maps are not meant to be a replacement for the relevant Ordinance Survey maps, (IE Explorer Series numbers 154, 155 and 167), but they do make it clear which paths are intended.

However, the fact that the maps depicted recognisable forms presented an additional complication and a bit of a problem. Some sort of explanation was called for, and, in **'Out from the Centre'**, some explanations were hurriedly brought into service. However, these were necessarily *ad hoc* explanations, and it was not until some weeks after the publication of the first book that the spiritual significance of the figures began to crystallise in my mind.

It would be better to pass over in silence the delusion that I was an unconscious practitioner of Feng Shui – an idea, which briefly came over me, when I read of similar figures in Sir James Fraser's **'Golden Bough'** – were it not for the happy accident that it pointed me in the direction of a collection of ancient philosophical sayings attributed to the Chinese sage, Lao Tzu.

A false trail led to the true path – as is often the case.

For me, a fruitless search for a copy of the Feng Shui bible, the **I-Ching** or **Book of Changes,** which I still believe is somewhere in the house, led me to a couple of translations of the **Tao Te Ching** left over from the 1970s[1].

The **Tao Te Ching,** traditionally attributed to Lao Tzu, is one of the pillars of the ancient philosophy (or religion) of

Taoism (or [2]Daoism) – of which the subject and object is the 'Tao', a word that means 'Path' (a fact that I knew from the '70s). Of course, I also knew that it means more than 'path' in the narrow sense of

a track across a field or a pavement alongside a road, but in order for the idea of a path to illuminate the rather obscure meaning of the Tao, there must be something in common between them. Consequently, it occurred to me that a book about paths might be able to throw some light on the Tao and vice versa. This has indeed proved to be the case, and a modern version of Taoism may yet prove to be a suitable creed for the post industrial society that must evolve if human beings are going to be part of the future of this planet. However, such a thoroughgoing reassessment of an ancient philosophy must wait for another book.

For the moment, I can only offer some extracts from the **Tao Te Ching** that may contribute to the contemplative attitude that adds to the enjoyment of a walk or a run in the countryside.

For the most part, these extracts, adopted from the two translations cited, have been chosen in relation to particular routes, or more often, in relation to the form that arose from the shape of the route on the map. It has to be said that it was easier to find a passage relevant to some routes than to others. But as the work progressed, I found that the succession of chapters deepened my understanding of the Tao and this has served to provide a kind of narrative connection between the routes. However, each of the circular 'paths' remain separate and the citations from the **Tao Te Ching** are only relevant to the individual routes, in the main.

On the other hand, one clause from the **Tao Te Ching** is specially relevant to all the routes in this book, namely: '*Returning is the motion of the Tao.*' This implies that a circular path is a particularly good model of the Tao. However, as it has been noted elsewhere, returning to ones starting point is not always easy:

Lao Tzu, Tao Te Ching, translated by D.C. Lau -1963 -Penguin Classics and Lao Tsu, Tao Te Ching, translated by Gia-Fu Feng and Jane English -1973 -Wildwood House, London
This is the preferred modern spelling, but I will keep the old spelling because it is more familiar.

An odd thing is a circular run
Its end is before it's begun.
If space/time is the way you roam
Irascibly away from home;
Beware, as budding Einsteins learn,
Such spiral routes brook no return!
When/where you hobble homeward, lame,
You'll find you can't; it's such a shame.
Though stamped your foot and ridged your brow,
You can't revisit here/<stroke>/now!

The Solution: - this is far from hard -
Don't set out from your own back yard!

This is a surprisingly Taoist response to a problem originally set by the ancient Greek philosopher, Heraklitus.

The **Tao Te Ching** also provides a useful summary of **the Country Code**, when it says:

A good walker leaves no tracks.

That covers the injunctions to **leave gates and property as you find them** and to **protect plants and animals and take your litter home**. The latter is the reason why you should **keep dogs under close control.**

The **Tao Te Ching** also reminds group leaders that:

The sage takes care of all men
And abandons no one.
He takes care of all things
And abandons nothing.

Nothing much more needs to be said on this subject, except to emphasize the necessity to take care of oneself. That means planning your trip into the countryside with care, using the necessary OS maps. Make sure you are fit enough to complete your journey and are wearing appropriate clothing. Carrying a mobile phone is also a good idea, provided it is turned off and is used only in emergencies!

The official Country Code (2007) expands the Taoist summary to read:

Be safe, plan ahead and follow any signs
Leave gates and property as you find them
Protect plants and animals and take your litter home
Keep dogs under close control
Consider other people

More details can be obtained from:
www.countrysideaccess.gov.uk

It is not possible to leave your house (or to remain in it) without some degree of risk; but there are some risks involved with a trip into the countryside, with which you may not be familiar. In my opinion, the most dangerous thing you are likely to meet is a motor car, especially if you wander unawares onto a minor road that is used as a rat run. I have indicated points, which I have found to be dangerous, but any piece of road can be deadly if there is a maniac driving down it! However, animals probably cause the greatest concern to most people.

As government advice has it:

'Wild animals and farm animals can behave unpredictably if you get too close, especially if they're with their young - so give them plenty of space.'

This is not always possible, and you may want animals, especially boisterous bullocks, to give you more space. Animals will not bother you if you are confident in your demeanour. Confidence can be improved by carrying a walking stick (which you must never actually use!) but your best defence is to keep along side a fence, so that frightened cattle are not cut off and can escape into the field without bumping into you.

Stout shoes and thick trousers will deal with most of the hazards caused by nettles and brambles on these routes, but there this is not practical if you are running and some routes are best left for the early spring, when vegetation has died back over the winter.

One or two places can be especially treacherous underfoot after rain, and I have been forced to wade on one occasion while following the Frome Valley Walkway.

However, none of these routes should be dangerous if you take sensible precautions.

Some people have questioned whether followers of the Path should drink alcohol. I am reassured by the history of Alan Watts, one of the leading exponents of eastern philosophy in the west who died in 1973. He was no stranger to alcohol and often lectured under its influence, with no loss of profundity according to witnesses. However, walks in the countryside involve a temptation to drink and drive, which must be resisted. The answer is to use public transport or marry someone who is willing to drive you from the pub. Otherwise, you need to belong to a group to share the burden. That could be an informal group of friends; or it might be a club, several of which can be found via:

www.closertothecountryside.co.uk

The trouble is: if you go out with a group, you are less likely to make contact with the community you are visiting, because all groups look inwards.

Such contradictions will have to remain unresolved for now; perhaps they will become disentangled at the end of **"The Path"**, which will be the third book in the series.

1: BEYOND THE AVON GORGE

OR 'RAGING BULL' 15 miles (approx.)

From the Observatory, beside the Suspension Bridge - ST566732

This route begins at the Observatory, a famous Bristol landmark beside the Clifton Suspension Bridge.

The Observatory has within it two means of seeing beyond the gorge. The first is a flight of steps leading down through a dark, rocky tunnel to a hermit's cave and a platform overhanging the sheer cliff of the gorge-side. The second is a camera obscura (literally a dark room) at the top of the tower, which projects panoramic images onto a curved table. These are typically Taoist ways of seeing, which make it possible to see beyond the gorge without leaving the Observatory.

As it is written in the Tao Te Ching:

> *Without going outside, you may know the whole world.*
> *Without looking through the window, you may see the ways of heaven.*
> *The further you go, the less you know.*
> *Thus the sage knows without travelling;*
> *He sees without looking.*

There are two other connections between the Observatory and Taoist traditions. Firstly, the fact that the cave below the Observatory used to be the home of a hermit, recalls the fact that Lao Tzu the author of the Tao Te Ching was also a hermit according to Chinese tradition.

Secondly, the situation of the Observatory - next to a toll bridge over a gorge on the western edge of Bristol - recalls the tradition that Lao Tzu was asked to write the Tao Te Ching by the Keeper of the Pass over the mountains on the western border of China.

At the same time, the Observatory forms the hidden eye of the raging bull, which has emerged like a primitive cave painting from the form of the sketch map of the route.

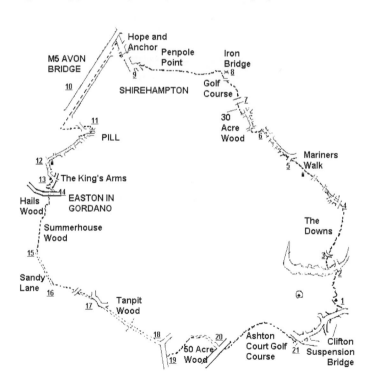

The sage in his hermitage can see the whole world in his mind's eye, but the rest of us need practice in following real paths before we can attempt such a feat.

All sages agree that the first step is to:

> *Empty yourself of everything.*
> *And let the mind rest at peace.*

I believe that the ideal way to accomplish this is a long walk or a steady run in the countryside, where the rhythm and flow of ones footsteps over varied terrain serve to distance the mind from the problems of the day by encouraging it to concentrate on the process of covering the ground.

The huge variety of terrain, grassland, parkland, woodland and farmland in this route makes it an attractive walk, if you have time to make the most of the scenery, and makes the miles fly by if you are running or training for a marathon.

If you are just beginning to take exercise, you may think that a fifteen mile route is too long for you at present. But be reassured that even:

> *A journey of a thousand miles begins under your feet.*

If you are walking, you will probably want to stop at the Hope and Anchor in Shirehampton or the Kings Arms in Easton in Gordano, where I have received a warm welcome in the past. But if you are running, you are likely to be more interested in the newsagent's next to the Hope and Anchor or the café on the golf course at Ashton Court, where you can obtain an isotonic fix, if you get your timing right.

There are several suitable pubs and cafés in Clifton that you can use when you return.

Parking is difficult during the week near the Suspension Bridge due to commuters from out of town. But bus services numbers 8, 8a, 9, 9a, 586 and 587 pass nearby.

Seasonal hazards: Brambles and nettles in 30 acre wood
Slippery under foot after rain in 50 acre wood

FROM THE OBSERVATORY TO KINGSWESTON HILL

To reach the Observatory (**1**) from Suspension Bridge Road, go up the tarmac path near the northeast chain of the Clifton Suspension Bridge.

This path goes past the Tailor's Friend, a sloping rock worn smooth by generations of trousered bottoms. No one could accuse it of being entirely safe.

If you are ready for it, follow the path to the left of the Observatory along the cliff-edge fence.

At the end of the clearing follow the path down to the right to emerge in the Promenade, an avenue of Beech Trees alongside a road.

Follow the Promenade down to Bridge Valley Road. **2**

Cross the road to 'Fountain Hill' opposite.

After about fifty metres, look out for a path on the left, and follow it through the trees to the cliff-side fence.

Turn right on the rocky path alongside the fence with the cliff on your left to emerge by a road. **3**

This is a peregrine viewpoint. I have never seen a peregrine falcon in the Avon Gorge, in spite of keeping my eyes open; but many have.

Cross the road on to the grass and go straight ahead, parallel with Ladies' Mile, for about 400m and then bear left along the avenue of trees across Clifton Down to Julian Road. **4**

Go down the right hand side of Julian Road to pick up Pitch and Pay Lane.

At the end of the lane, cross a road and descend Mariners' Walk past Stoke Bishop Church (Beware of loose rocks underfoot!) to Sneyd Park Road. **5**

Turn right then left on a short footpath through some trees.

Keep left along a short stretch of road without a footpath. When you regain pavement, keep straight on across three roads until you reach the River Trym. **6**

Cross the river and turn left along the grass on the far bank.

Follow the river downstream until fifty metres before a weir, then turn right to find a path between some brambles into a cul-de-sac.

Turn right when you reach the road and follow it round to the left

past a school and a church and turn left again down Avonleaze.
Look for a narrow footpath on the right, which leads through the brambles of Thirty Acre Wood past the backs of some houses to emerge on Sylvan Way. **7**

Cross the road onto Shirehampton Golf Course. Then follow the right-hand fence up the hill around the greens to a kissing gate onto Shirehampton Road.

Cross the road and climb the grassy bank opposite to some steps with the Iron Bridge to your right. **8**

FROM THE IRON BRIDGE TO THE KING'S ARMS

Go up the steps onto a track in the Kingsweston House estate. On the track, turn left and follow it under the trees to a cross-track. Turn right between some boulders and then left along another track.

A backward glance before you disappear among the trees will give you a view of Kingsweston House (designed by Vanbrough) across the grass.

Keep on the track until you emerge in a grassy clearing on a ridge (Penpole Point).

Go straight ahead past a circular stone seat and a trig point and descend some irritating rustic steps to a road. *I do not understand why people insist on installing these steps. They seem to me to make the descent more dangerous.*

On the road, turn left and follow the pavement on the right down to a major road (Lower High Street, Shirehampton). **9**
Cross the road and turn right towards the M5 motorway flyover. *You pass the Hope and Anchor and a newsagent's shop, which provide two rare opportunities for refreshment on this route.*

17

Just before the flyover, turn left up the cycle/footpath across the River Avon. **10**

Descend from the M5 Bridge and continue along the cycle/footpath, under a new railway bridge to look for a tunnel under the old railway on the right. **11**

Through the tunnel, turn right on a road.

As the road bends sharply to the left take the track on the right, which loops round behind some houses to another road.

In this road, turn right and follow it to a T-junction.

At the junction turn right and follow the road, past Easton-in-Gordano Church to another T-junction. **12**

Turn left and carry on to yet another T-junction, next to the Kings' Arms. **13**

FROM THE KING'S ARMS TO BRUNEL'S BRIDGE

At the junction, turn right, and as the road bends sharply to the right cross the road into Martcombe Road opposite.

Go up the road, which becomes a path to a major road ahead. **14**

Cross the road and turn right along the pavement, looking for a stile into the field on the left.

Over the stile, go up the wood-side, looking for a stile into the wood on the right.

Over the stile, descend the path to a track along the side of a stream.

The stream bed is actually a bridle path, although fallen trees make it unlikely that it is often used for that purpose. It makes a good paddle if you fancy one!

To keep dry feet, turn left along the streamside path and continue to a stile into a field.

Over the stile, turn right and follow the path through the field to a pair of stiles beside a wood.

Go straight ahead until the path enters a wood along a track that can be very muddy, even when other places are dry.

When you emerge into another field, follow the stream on your right to a kissing gate and continue to follow the stream, looking for a plank-bridge over it and a stile into the drive beside a house. **15**

Turn left and follow Sandy Lane uphill until you come to a footpath on the left, which leads up the drive of another house to a stile. **16**

Over the stile, go slightly right of straight ahead to a stile by a gate in the far top corner of the field.

Over the stile, go straight across the road to a concrete track, which descends to emerge onto a road beside Mulberry Farm. **17**

Turn right and keep to the road as it bends sharply to the left. Around the bend, look for a stony track on the right.

Follow the track for about three-quarters of a mile over the hill to a road. **18**

Go straight up the road to a gap into the bottom of Fifty Acre Wood on the left. **19**

Follow the muddy cycle path along the lower edge of the wood to emerge onto an ascending track.

Turn right and go uphill onto a metalled lane.

Go straight ahead past some houses on the left to a major road. It is a bit of a rat-run. **20**

Turn left and then right through a gap in the wall.

Through the gap, go straight on through trees onto a golf course.

Bear left towards the clubhouse, watching out for golf balls. Pass to the right of the clubhouse and continue on the same line to the lodge gates out of Ashton Court Estate. **21**

Cross the main road and Bridge Road by the pedestrian crossings.

Turn right and follow the road to Clifton Suspension Bridge. (The Forest Path does a loop through the houses to skirt Leigh Woods at this point, but I cannot really see the point, unless you actually wish to visit the woods.)

Cross the Suspension Bridge and enjoy the view!

As you near the Clifton side of the bridge, take a careful look at the rocks around the platform sticking out from the cliff. You should be able to make out the outlines of the windows of the hermitage. When the hermit lived in the cave, he did not have the benefit of the tunnel from the Observatory. He had to scale the cliff to gain his solitary retreat. Effort is required to achieve the detachment of a sage. You may feel, on completing this route that you have earned the right to visit the observatory!

2: THE WILD WEST

OR 'THE DIVING BEAR' 7.5 or 8.5 miles (approx.)

From the Blaise Inn in Henbury -ST562788

This route begins at the Blaise Inn in Henbury, whose inn sign carries the picture of another hermit, St Blaise, an Armenian bishop, hermit and martyr. According to his legend, he was a healer of men and of beasts, which gathered round his cave. He was arrested as a Christian by huntsmen seeking animals for the arena. He healed a boy choking on a fish bone on his way to prison. His persecutors could not drown him in a lake, because the water supported him, so they tortured him with wool combs and beheaded him. (I think I would have preferred drowning; but how can you be sure?) His associations with wild animals and water link him to the figure of a Diving Bear, which has appeared in the sketch map of the route. He is also associated with diseases of the throat, due to the fishbone.
The route passes through two nature reserves, Lawrence Weston Moor and Kingsweston Down. On other parts of the

21

route, I have come across buzzards wheeling overhead, snipe springing from the ditches of St Bede's playing field and deer slots in a nearby wood. Even the bank alongside the motorway is richly endowed with wildflowers in the spring.

However, the area is also wild in the Wild West sense, and you may come across youths armed with air rifles hunting rabbits near Berwick Lodge and on Kingsweston Down, who would remind St Blaise of the huntsmen who seized him. The men you may see armed with shotguns under the motorway bridge are clay-pigeon shooters from Mount Skitham and you may also spot paint-ballers at Berwick Lodge Farm.

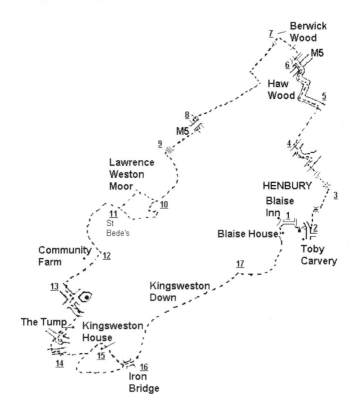

If your throat needs relief on the way round, there is a tea room in the vaults of Kingsweston House, and there is the Hope and Anchor over the road at the turnaround point on the longer route. If your throat is still dry back at the pub, I recommend the Taunton Traditional rough cider. If you want to eat, or prefer blander drink, you will need to go around the corner to the Toby Carvery at the Salutation[3] or to the café in the Blaise Estate.

There is little or no parking at the pub, so park around the corner at the Blaise estate car park or near the Salutation, if you are driving. If you are not driving, the number 1, 43, 77 and 624 buses all stop nearby.

Seasonal hazards: Brambles and nettles around Lawrence Weston Moor, especially where the railway crosses the M5.

THE BLAISE INN TO BERWICK LODGE

Starting with your back to the pub **1**, turn right and then left into a cobbled lane down to the church. Turn right into the churchyard and then take the path to the left of the church.

It is hard to miss the colourful grave of Scipio Africanus near the church. A little further on the grave of a lady archaeologist is marked by the pagan Egyptian symbol of the ankh.

Go down the steps at the end of the church and follow the road to the ford. **2**

Cross the road to a stone stile and continue along the bank of the stream to a bridge. Cross the bridge and turn left. (The second left along the flood-bank is the easier path.) Follow the path to a bridge back across the stream. **3**

Over the bridge, take the right hand of two metalled paths into a cul-de-sac, at the other end of which turn right and look for a Community Forest Path sign on the left, beside a pedestrian snicket.

For some reason, the Community Forest Path continues alongside the stream for a hundred yards and loops back to this point, but that seems an unnecessary complication.

3 The Salutation is a shortened version of a traditional pub name, 'The Angel's Salutation' - IE Hail Mary, the Angel's Salutation to the Virgin Mary. The name is also shortened to the Angel.

Follow the path across another cul-de-sac to a main road. Cross the road and turn right. Take the first turning on the left and follow the right hand pavement to a T-junction.

This area rejoices in the curious name, Botany Bay, but I have no idea what its connection is with the Australian penal colony of the same name!

Go straight on across a road to a railway bridge and a kissing gate into a field. **4**

In the field, turn right and follow the fence on the right to another kissing gate into a horse field. Keep going in the same direction through another kissing gate and through a wicket gate onto Berwick Lane beside Norton Farm. **5**

Turn left and follow the lane up the hill past Haw Wood and over the motorway. **6**

There is a splendid view down the motorway towards Avonmouth. Some people do not like industrial scenery, but, as it says in the Tao Te Ching:

> *Under heaven, all can see beauty as beauty,*
> *Only because there is ugliness.*

Go past the quad-bike track on the right to a crossroads. Turn right and look for a kissing gate on the left. Go through the gate into a rough field.

This is where I once met a youth with an air rifle out after rabbits.

Go straight ahead, avoiding boggy patches as best you can, past a pond and a wood on your left to find a substantial double stile and bridge in the corner of the field leading into the grounds of Berwick Lodge. **7**

FROM BERWICK LODGE TO LAWRENCE WESTON MOOR

Turn left and pick your way through the bulbs or nettles (depending on the season) to the entrance to the Lodge off Berwick Lane. Go straight ahead over a stile and follow the right hand hedge to a kissing gate into another field.

Follow the right hand hedge *(which conceals a paint-balling wood)* to the corner of the field. Turn left and follow the track to a gate. Go straight ahead over a stile (it can be boggy on the other side) and make your way down slope to the motorway fence.

Follow the motorway fence for about 600m to a stile into a field.

The bank beside the fence is full of wildflowers in spring.

The right of way is supposed to follow the motorway fence, but it is obstructed by brambles, so you must climb the bank on the right and continue parallel to the fence until you can approach a small stile. Go over the stile into a paddock and look for a wooden kissing gate in the corner of the field.

Turn left under the motorway-bridge. **8**

This is where the men with the shot guns park to go clay-pigeon shooting.

Look for the steps on the right at the other end of tunnel and climb up to a kissing gate into a field. Go straight on parallel to the motorway, through a gap to a stile below a railway line. Turn right and follow the path beside the motorway under the railway-bridge into a field. (Beware of brambles encroaching onto the path.) **9**

I notice that people without the means to hack their way through the brambles tend to trespass on the railway bank at this point, a course of action that it is impossible to recommend; but what are they to do? I wonder whose responsibility it is to keep such paths open. One problem is that the railway line is the boundary between Bristol and South Gloucestershire, but I suspect that the railway company has some thing to do with it.

LAWRENCE WESTON MOOR TO KINGSWESTON RIDGE

In the field, turn left and head for a gap in the hedge ahead, next to the railway line.

Through the hedge, turn right and head for the diagonally opposite corner of an old field. Cross the relatively solid ditch between two oak trees and then go straight ahead across another similar ditch and on towards a stile.

Over the stile, go straight ahead over another stile and go up to a kissing gate onto a wooden bridge.

Instead of going through the kissing gate, turn right along a mown path through the reeds towards a pond. **10**

This path gives access to the Lawrence Moor Nature Reserve for the children of Bank Leaze Primary School. There are paths through the Nature Reserve, which you will have to use because the path around the school playing field is generally blocked by brambles.

Pass to the left of the pond and look for a kissing gate on the left.

Lawrence Weston Moor is the last remaining fragment of the marshland that used to stretch from the Blaise Estate to the mouth of the Avon. It is crisscrossed with rhines, as the drainage ditches of South Gloucestershire and Somerset are called. This is a rich environment for rare species.

As it is written in the Tao Te Ching:

> *Water gives life to the 10 000 things.*
> *It flows in places men reject, and so is like the Tao.*

Through the gate, turn right and head for another kissing gate straight ahead.

Through the gate, follow the left hand hedge until you can turn left along a farm track.

Keep going straight ahead along the track until you come to a crossroads. (You may need to go through two sets of kissing gates if the field gates are shut.)

At the crossroads, go straight ahead and then right alongside the playing fields. **11**

It is possible to get across the playing fields, where I have seen snipe rising, but there is no right of way.

Follow the path between the playing fields and the motorway, which emerges in an open area of scrub.

Turn left before you reach a sewage pumping station and follow the path past the Community Farm to emerge on the Lawrence Weston Greenway cycle path. **12**

Turn right to follow the path until it comes out in Campbell's Drive.

Turn right and then left along Kings Weston Lane **13** towards a roundabout.

EXTENSION (an extra mile, approximately)

You could instead cross over Kings Weston Lane **13** and continue along the cycle path to the end.

Turn left to emerge in Shirehampton's Lower High Street. **14a**

Turn left and cross Kings Weston Avenue by the traffic lights. *Unless you wish to visit the Hope and Anchor first.*

Turn left up Penpole Lane **15a** and as the lane bends to the right, go straight ahead down a back lane and turn immediately right up some rustic steps onto Penpole Ridge.

Take the left hand fork past the trig point and continue till you emerge within sight of Kingsweston House, where you rejoin the main routes.

This option has the advantage of an opportunity to stop for a pint at the Hope and Anchor in Lower High Street, but it produces an image of a bear that reminds us that omnivores also eat red meat.

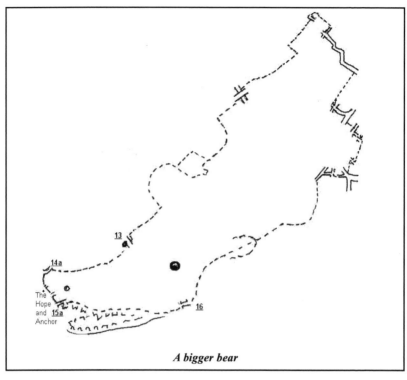

A bigger bear

Otherwise:

At the roundabout, turn right and then left up Moor Grove.

Look for a metalled footpath of the right.

Follow the footpath around 'The Tump' until you reach a barrier at the exit from the green space.

If you take the left hand exit along the pavement, you will be on the right line to cross Barrowmead Avenue and Moorend Gardens towards a children's playground.

Turn left, just before the play equipment and follow the path up the field to a road.

Turn left along the road and look for a footpath between the houses on the right. **14**

Turn left in the wood and follow path disfigured by litter and dumped household goods along the backs of the houses until it climbs up a gravelled drive with a view of Kingsweston House to the left. **15**

Kingsweston House was designed by Vanbrough, whilst he was developing the skills he needed to design a much grander project - Castle Howerd in Yorkshire.

If you are going to make use of the tearooms, follow the drive to the left of the house. The Vaulted Tearooms are marked by an awning.

If you do not want tea, cut across the grass to join the drive from the house to a Roman folly at the top of the hill.

Behind the folly are some steps, which emerge near the Iron Bridge **16** onto the path along the crest of Kingsweston Ridge.

KINGSWESTON RIDGE TO THE BLAISE INN

From the Iron Bridge, go straight ahead along the ridge of Kingsweston Down.

At the end of the Down **17**, descend the steps beyond the remains of a kissing gate across a muddy track and out onto the grass.

Go straight ahead to the tracks leading into the wood opposite.

Take the middle stony track, which climbs most steeply upwards to the folly, known as Blaise Castle in the clearing at the top. (The real castle is the hill fort, hidden in the trees, which surrounds the sham.)

Turn right to Lovers' Leap, just before you reach the folly and descend the path past a cave, most suitable for a hermit. When the path emerges toward the top of a metalled drive, turn left and follow the drive past Blaise House to leave the estate onto the road, opposite the Blaise Inn.

3: RHINELAND
OR 'THE RAVEN' from 6 to 12 miles (approx.)
From the Fox at Easter Compton ST572824

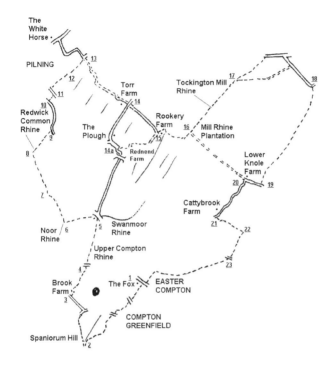

It is said in the Tao Te Ching:
  A great country is like low land.
  It is the meeting ground of the Universe.

*The Raven depicted in the map is flying over low land,
which would be an extensive marsh were it not for the fact
that it is crisscrossed by rhines, as drainage ditches are
called in South Gloucestershire and Somerset. When we
climb Spaniorum Hill, to obtain a raven's eye view, we can
see why it might be called the meeting ground of the
Universe.*

31

The distance is dominated by the two modern road bridges over the Severn Estuary carrying the M4 and M48 motorways.

The nearer, left-hand bridge is the most recent, and stands on the site of the New Passage to Wales. This began as a stage coach crossing until the coming of steam engines turned it into the terminus of a railway line linked to a ferry. This in turn was replaced by a Victorian railway tunnel. You would expect any tunnel under water to carry a risk of flooding, but the problems that were encountered here were not under the estuary but in Wales, where an underground river was unexpectedly encountered, and a few cracks in the English Stones, a reef that is only covered by high tides.

The older suspension bridge over the Severn replaced the Aust Ferry, which was a car ferry in its last incarnation. However, the ferry was an ancient institution. Aust is a contraction of Augustine and it was so called because it was the site of a famous meeting between St Augustine and the bishops of Wales who had come across the ferry to meet him. The saint's purpose was to persuade the Welsh bishops to join him in his attempt to convert the pagan English. At the time the chief god of the English and the ancestor of all the English Kings (save one) was Woden, whose sacred bird, the Raven whispered prophecies in his ear.

The saint failed, because the Welsh bishops had taken the advice of a Welsh hermit, who suggested they should arrive late and see whether he rose to greet them as brothers or remained seated like a king. He stayed in his seat, which was taken as evidence that the saint was guilty of the deadly sin of pride.

Lao Tzu had a similar attitude to the famous Chinese philosopher Confucius, to whom he said, according to tradition: 'Rid yourself of your arrogance and your lustfulness, your ingratiating manners and your excessive ambition. These are all detrimental to your person. This is all I have to say to you.'

Don't we all know somebody we would like to say that to!
When the Raven reported back to Woden, the failure of the
meeting must have sounded like good news to the pagan god.

The full route, starting from the Fox at Easter Compton is
at least ten and a half miles, rather longer if you divert to
visit the Cross Hands, the White Horse or the Plough en
route. On the other hand, it is possible to shorten the route
considerably by removing a wing or a tail, although that
does not do the Raven any favours! The Plough is currently
the highest rated pub in Pilning, although I like the cider at
the White Horse.
The Fox, which serves some excellent real ale, is a stop on
the 624 and 625 bus services from Old Market, Clifton Down,
Westbury, etc., but the service is infrequent, so it is advisable
to check with the operators, the South Gloucestershire Bus
and Coach company if you intend to use it.

Seasonal Hazards: Nettles and Hemlock at 16
Nettles between 22 and 23
Cattle and horses

THE RAVEN'S HEAD

From the Fox **1**, turn right along the road, and look for a footpath
on the right, past the village hall and the verger's cottage.

Follow the path through the field towards the parish church. *Note the Norman style arch in the porch.*

Make your way through the graveyard onto the road on the other side.

Go through the kissing gate opposite, and follow the left hand hedge to another kissing gate.

Bear right to another kissing gate leading to a path onto the road at Compton Greenfield.

Turn right and look for steps on the left, which lead to yet another kissing gate and a path beside an orchard.

Through the kissing gate at the top of the orchard, follow the left hand hedge to another kissing gate.

Pause and look back before you go through the gate to enjoy the view of the second Severn Crossing.

On the other side, follow the left hand hedge to a wicket gate set in a large field gate. Do not be tempted by the right hand path, which is not a right of way.

There is perhaps a better view back to the second Severn Crossing in this field.

Go diagonally right up the steep slope, which is strewn with wildflowers in the spring, to find a kissing gate in the far corner of the field *(Eg Cinquefoil, self-heal, oxeye daisy, birdsfoot trefoil. I remember cowslips, but I was too late to see any on my last visit. There is an excellent sighting of the original motorway bridge, framed by the trees on the right at the top of the bank.)*

In the next field, go straight ahead to a new kissing gate, leading into a fenced track. **2** *This track leads to the site of a new scouting centre.*

Turn right down the track to pick up the footpath through a horse gate on the right, just after a small wood.

The track leads down to Spaniorum Farm, which is famous for its gym, the base of a number of local boxers.

Descend to a stile in the diagonally opposite corner of the field.

Go straight on to find the next stile on the left past the arena.

Bear right to a stile onto a minor road.

In the road, turn right and then left up Vimpenny's Lane.

3 Turn right up a drive to Brook Farm (at the end on the right; Elmtree Farm is named on the gate ahead.)

Do not enter Elmtree Farm. Instead, go through the gate on the left alongside the brook.

Turn right through a gate into a field.

There is no exit from the field on the line of the path as marked on the Explorer map. Instead, bear left to the gate next to Lyde Brook.

Follow the brook on your left to a stile onto a lane. **4** *(This is National Cycle Route 4. The last time I used it, we were surprised by a speeding motorcycle!)*

Go through the gate opposite and then immediately left through another gate.

Turn right and go straight across the field to a bridge across Upper Compton Rhine.

Go straight across the next field to another bridge.

Go diagonally across the next field to emerge in the far corner onto the main road.

This is marked on the map as Swanmoor Bridge over the Swanmoor Rhine. **5**

FIRST SHORTCUT (cuts off about 2 miles)

To avoid the Raven's Wing, cross the road (**5**) and go down Station Road. *The stone wall on your right is part of Swanmoor Bridge over the eponymous rhine.*

After about a kilometre, the road goes under a railway line.

As the road zigzags past a track to Pilning Station on the left, look for the drive to Rednend Farm on the right **14a**

[If you want to visit the Plough, it is a couple of hundred metres further up the road past the turning to Pilning.

To rejoin the main route, either: continue up the road to Awkley and Olveston to a crossroads past Torr Farm, where you should turn right. 14

Or: return to the drive to Rednend Farm 14a.]

Look for a footbridge into the field on the left before you reach the farm.

Over the stile, turn right and follow the rhine on your right to the end of the field.

Turn right using the footbridge over the rhine and make your way to a stile onto a track.

Turn left and follow the track to Rookery Farm. **15**

Follow the drive past a barking dog to the left of the farm.

Otherwise:

Turn left without crossing the road and immediately left again into a sports field.

Head for a stile in the diagonally opposite corner of the field. It may be better going around the left hand edge of the field if it is still as overgrown as it was on my last visit.

Turn left through a gap in the shelter belt and head for a footbridge over the rhine in the far right corner of the field. **6**

Turn right to a gate over the Noor Rhine and follow the right hand hedge to another gate.

The footpath is shown on the other side of the hedge, but this route is impassable.

Continue straight ahead through a gap and look for a gate on your right past a power line. **7**

Over the gate, turn left to a series of three stiles onto a farm track and three more descending on the other side.

Go straight ahead with a hedge on your left to a bridge and a stile, followed by a bridge with a stile at either end.

Continue straight ahead past two gates on your left and a rhine ahead. **8**

Turn right and follow Redwick Common Rhine until you emerge via a grassy/muddy track onto the main road. **9**

Cross the road and turn left along the pavement into Pilning. You will cross the main line from London to Wales on its way to the Severn Tunnel.

About three hundred and fifty metres further on, you will come to a footpath between the houses on the right. **10** [the **Cross Hands Inn is 200 metres further on**]

As you emerge onto a lane (**11**), *you will pass some allotments, which have been established on the line of a disused railway, which used to lead to the New Passage ferry across the Severn.*

Turn left and look for a gate into a field on the right after about a hundred metres.

Follow the right hand edge of the field alongside a rhine to a gate a few metres from the corner of the field.

Carry on across the next field to a bridge over the rhine in the corner of the field. **12**

The right of way goes over the bridge, not over the gate ahead.

Over the bridge, turn left and follow the left hand hedge through a gate and through the next field to emerge over a stile built into the gate into a lane or track. **13**

WHITE HORSE (adds about a mile)

To visit the White Horse, turn left to emerge on a road.

Turn left along the road and after about four hundred metres, turn right over the motorway.

On the far side, turn left to find the White Horse at the end of a cul-de-sac. Return to the track the same way as you came.

NB: There is another route at www.closertothecountryside.co.uk, which explores the rhines and railways from the White Horse. It is called River Horse.

Otherwise:
Turn right along the track and stay on it (keeping left past the entrance to Gumhurn Farm) until you emerge on a road beside Torr Farm. **14**

THE PLOUGH (adds about half a mile)

If you wish to visit the Plough, turn right and follow the road for about seven hundred metres to find the Plough on your left.

When you emerge, turn left and follow the road towards the railway line.

As the road bends look for the footpath up the drive of Rednend Farm on the left. **14a**

Look for a footbridge into the field on the left before you reach the farm.

Over the stile, turn right and follow the rhine on your right to the end on the field.

Turn right using the footbridge over the rhine and make your way to a stile onto a track.

Turn left and follow the track to Rookery Farm. **15**

Follow the drive past a barking dog to the left of the farm.

Otherwise:

Go straight on over the crossroads and carry on for about six hundred metres to Rookery Farm. **15**

Turn left along the drive past a barking dog on the near side of the farm.

[This is where the detour to the Plough rejoins the main route.]

The dog sounds fierce, but it is chained up and wags its tail as you pass. The cars you may see to the left belong to the Hayes Independent Hospital, a secure unit run by the National Autistic Society.

Go straight ahead though two gates through the farmyard.

Continue straight ahead along a track beside a rhine into a field.

Turn right alongside the hedge to a gate.

In the next field, the right of way bears left across the field, according to the map, but you will find no stile, only a yellow mark on a tree. Instead go straight ahead to a gate.

Bear left across the next field to a gate in the opposite corner, next to Tockington Mill Rhine.

Go through the gate and follow the rhine to a gate in the next corner (ignoring the footbridge over the rhine).

16 Over the gate, fight your way through the hemlock and nettles onto a track. *Yes that is the same hemlock that was used to kill Socrates. You can recognise hemlock as a tall version of cow parsley with purple blotches on the stem. So take care not to get any in your mouth!*

On the other side of the track is the corner of Mill Rhine Plantation, which is part of a new wood on Lower Knole Farm. This is the biggest of the new woods that have been planted as part of the Forest of Avon initiative.

SECOND SHORTCUT (cuts off about 2.5 miles)
To avoid the Raven's Tail, turn right along the green lane.

[Or go into the wood and turn right on the permissive path alongside the green lane.

Rejoin the lane through a gate on your right, when your way is blocked by Middle Rhine, and turn left.]

Past Lower Knole Farm, turn right along a minor road. **20**

THE RAVEN'S TAIL
Otherwise:

Go straight ahead alongside Tockington Mill Rhine.

The path crosses four field boundaries before it reaches the junction of Tockington Mill Rhine with Bunsham Rhine to the left and Sandy Rhine to the right. **17**

Turn right over a stile beside a gate into the field beyond the end of the shelter belt.

Follow Sandy Rhine, on your right until you reach a horse gate up the bank to the right of a field gate.

Follow the enclosed track past a wood to a gate onto a minor road.

When the road bends sharply to the left, go straight ahead over a stile to the left of a gate. **18**

Bear right across the field to find a double stile and footbridge to the right of a rickety field gate.

Follow the left hand hedge through a couple of gateways and over a pair of stiles until you emerge in a farm track.

Go straight ahead to a sharp bend to the right, where you must continue straight ahead over a stile beside a gate into a field.

Continue to follow the left hand hedge through a series of gateways until you reach a gate beside a wood.

Continue straight ahead, but be aware of the electric fence in front of it.

Continue straight on alongside the wood. When the grassy strip opens out, look out for an electric horse fence across the path.

Go straight ahead to a stile next to the field gate onto a minor road. **19**

Turn right.

Keep to the road as it bends sharply to the left opposite Knole Farm. **20**

[The Second Shortcut rejoins the main route at this point.]

Follow the lane through Cattybrook Farm to a railway tunnel.

The tall chimney on the left belongs to Cattybrook Brick Works. This works was established as part of the project to build a railway tunnel under the Severn. You will see that some of the bricks have been used in the farm buildings. The tunnel under the railway embankment is particularly impressive and looks as though the engineers practised on it to hone their skills for the main tunnel under the Severn to the west.

THE RETURN

On the other side of the tunnel, turn left through a gate past a pair of cottages. **21**

Follow the left hand edge of the field, where you may hear running water in the vegetation alongside the embankment.

At the top end of the field, go over the stile marked "Beware of the dog". *(The dog was so old that it was unaware of our presence until we had passed it.)*

Follow the drive past a series of bungalows to a road beside a footbridge over the railway line. **22**

This bridge leads to a convenient footpath from Lower Knole Farm, but there is no right of way over it. This seems to be a general rule with convenient footbridges over railway lines.

Turn right.

When the lane bends sharply to the left, go straight on down an enclosed path.

(You are now back on the Community Forest Path.)

Go over a stile onto another section of enclosed path, which emerges in a lane opposite a house.

The Forest Path continues, somewhat disconcertingly through the garden of the house. **23**

In the field, go straight ahead to a gate beside a gap.

The next field always seems to be full of long grass when I try to go through it. There are often mown strips alongside the fields in the next section, but these are part of the set aside regime, so they do not actually follow a useful line, from a walker's point of view.

You need to head for a new gate (concealing the rickety stile that it replaced) in the diagonally opposite corner.

Through the gate, look for a bridge, guarded by a pair of gates on your left.

In the next field, bear right to a pair of stiles and a bridge beside a wooden telegraph pole. *There is also a dead tree that looks a little like a rhinoceros from some angles, just before the bridge.*

41

In the next field, keep going straight ahead on the same line to another pair of stiles and a bridge.

The path in the next field is much easier to follow as it is within regular dog-walking distance of Easter Compton. *I should imagine dog-walkers use the mown strips around the other fields, as they do not have to go anywhere in particular.*

There is another stiled bridge in the far corner of the field, leading into a wood.

This is another wood planted under the auspices of the Forest of Avon.

In the wood, bear right at a junction to emerge through a kissing gate onto a farm track.

Cross over to another kissing gate and follow the left hand hedge to a pair of stiles and a bridge, which emerges opposite a skate board park.

Turn left and follow the track alongside a play ground to emerge onto the road in Easter Compton.

The Fox is about fifty metres to the right on the opposite side of the road.

4: IGNORING THE ALMONDSBURY INTERCHANGE

OR 'MENACING BEAKER' from 7 to 11 miles (approx.)

From the Leisure Centre in Bradley Stoke ST623820

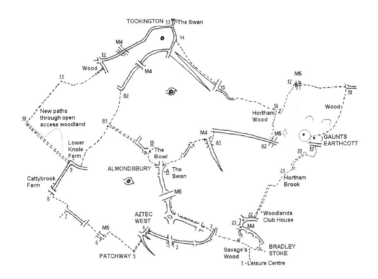

Beaker was the fictional assistant of scientist, Dr Bunsen Honeydew, in the Muppet Show (1976-1982). In every episode, Beaker would end up the victim of the bland scientist's experiments. Here a bizarre genetic experiment seems to have backfired on the unfortunate assistant.

This nightmare vision has come about through an attempt to find rural footpaths around one of the busiest motorway junctions in the region, where the M4 from London to Cardiff and Southwest Wales crosses the M5 from Birmingham to Exeter and the Cornish Peninsular. So, the most obvious passage to apply seems to be:

The universe is sacred.
You cannot improve it.
If you try to change it, you will ruin it.
If you try to hold it, you will lose it.

However, the word universe belongs to the translator - the
original Chinese is more usually rendered 'empire' - so its
application to this figure is problematic.
In any case, the first route in this group was the 'Beaker'
route from the Swan in Almondsbury, which was devised to
make use of a footbridge over the M5. The stork and the
elephants were added later. So it may be that Beaker is
getting away with it. In which case, we should take note that:

> *He who is filled with virtue is like a newborn babe.*
> *Wasps and serpents will not sting him*
> *Wild beasts will not pounce on him*
> *Birds of prey will not attack him*
> *His bones are soft, and his sinews supple*
> *But his grip is firm*
> *He has not experienced the union of man and*
> *woman,*
> *But his male member is in working order*
> *He howls all day without becoming hoarse*
> *This is perfect harmony.*

That is Beaker to a T (or any other teenage geek); but the
comparison between the man of virtue and a new born babe
seems to be taken to an extreme that suggests that the
passage may have a satirical intention, although strenuous
efforts have been made by scholars to take it seriously.

The main route starts from the Leisure Centre in Bradley Stoke, but it would work equally well from the Travellers Rest in Patchway or the Swan Inn in Tockington. The lesser routes bring in the Swan and the Bowl at Almondsbury.

At the time of writing, the best pub in Bradley Stoke is the Three Brooks near the Leisure Centre.

The 71 bus from Bristol and the 574 from Filton Abbey Wood and Parkway Stations terminate at the Bradley Stoke Tesco near the Leisure Centre; the 73B passes it, as does the 483 from Yate to Cribbs Causeway, and the 73 and 73A pass nearby in Brook Road. The 73s also pass the Travellers' Rest, as do the 309, 310 and 312 to Thornbury, which also stop near the Swan at Almondsbury.

Known Hazards: Concealed rat run between 6 and 7 Brambles and nettles beyond Hortham Wood and along Hortham Brook

---

FROM THE LEISURE CENTRE TO PRIMROSE BRIDGE

Coming out of the entrance of the leisure centre **1**, turn left and make your way to the cycle path at the far side of the car park. Turn left alongside the edge of Savage's Wood, where you will see catkins and teasels in the appropriate season.

Keep left at the bottom of the hill and enter the wood. (There is a choice of kissing gate or stile!)

Keep straight on through the wood as much as you can. At one point you need to bear right over a bridge in the wood.

When you emerge into the open, keep going straight on, alongside the Patchway Brook. Ignore the first bridge on your right near a new pond and carry on through the gap in the cut and laid hedge.

Keep going until you reach a footbridge overhead **2**.

FROM PRIMROSE BRIDGE TO THE ALMONDSBURY SWAN

If you intend to do one of the shorter versions of the route, carry on under the footbridge **2** and follow the path alongside Bradley Stoke Way to the Aztec West Roundabout. (You will need to go past a roundabout and a set of traffic lights on the way. At Aztec West Roundabout, turn right and follow the footpath under the motorway. (Take care -the traffic won't!) Carry on past the Almondsbury Parish Hall, Sports and Social Centre until you reach the Swan **A**.

FROM PRIMROSE BRIDGE TO LOWER KNOLE FARM

Turn right, using the small footbridge over the Patchway Brook and make your way left up to the higher footbridge.

Turn left over the footbridge and follow the road known as the Common across one cross road and on to the Gloucester Road. **3** *The Travellers' Rest (a Hungry Horse Pub) is off to the right at this point. This would make a good alternative starting point for the main route.*

Turn left to find the underpass to the other side and then make your way to Hempton Lane.

Follow the lane to the end where there are steps up onto Park Avenue on the Aztec West Estate and turn left. **4**

Take the second turning on the left (Waterside Drive) and the first right beside the lake.

Immediately you have left the trading estate, turn right into the Tumps nature area. **5**

Follow the right hand fence all the way to the side of the motorway, where the path forces you to turn left. After a few yards, you will find a footbridge on your right (which rejoices in the name of 'The Banana Bridge'. **6**

Cross the footbridge and carry on through Pegwell Brake and past a plant nursery to Over Lane. Take care; there can be a lot of fast traffic on this lane!

Turn left and then right down Ash Lane.

After about a kilometre, the lane bends to the right, leaving the community Forest Path. **7**

Just before you reach a footbridge over the railway line (no right of way), turn left up the shared drive of some houses to emerge at a stile into a field.

Follow the right hand edge of the field past a hidden stream beside the railway line and past some cottages onto a minor road. **8**

Turn right under the railway bridge and carry on through Cattybrook Farm to a bend to the right at Lower Knole Farm. **9**

FROM LOWER KNOLE FARM TO THE ALMONDSBURY SWAN

Carry on round the bend **(9)** to the right and look for a stile next to a gate. In the field, go straight ahead to the corner of a wood, where there was an electric horse fence across a narrow strip of grass the last time I visited. Carry on to a gate.

Through the gate, watch out for another electric fence and go straight ahead along the hedge on your right.

Negotiate three gates, which are usually open, or the stiles next to them until you reach a stile next to a gate onto a farm track. **B1**

Follow the track round the bend to the right and up the hill to a stile next to a gate.

Go straight ahead to a road and carry straight on up Church Road.

Turn left, just before the church toward the Bowl Inn. **B**

The footpath on the right goes through the churchyard, just before the inn. Follow the path, which emerges between two stone gateposts at a road junction.

Turn left along a dotted line to a tarmac footpath through the trees up Almondsbury Hill to a road.

It is well worth making a detour to the parking space, fifty metres to the right, which commands splendid views of the bridges over the Severn Estuary. If the light is right, the New Bridge looks especially magical.

Retrace your steps and cross the A38 toward the Swan with great care and turn left (unless you wish to visit the pub). **A**

FROM LOWER KNOLE FARM TO THE TOCKINGTON SWAN VIA TOCKINGTON MILL RHINE

At the bend, turn left up a green lane and follow it for about three-quarters of a mile alongside the new plantations on your right until the end of the track, where it opens out between two gates (the one on the left is often concealed by a hemlock). **10**

It is possible to follow several permissive paths through the wood. The simplest runs parallel to the green lane from Middle Rhine (about 700m along the lane) to the end of the track. Unfortunately there is no way across Tockington Mill Rhine.

Turn right over a gate and negotiate a series of gates alongside the Tockington Mill Rhine which follows the wood on the right for about two-thirds of a mile.

At the end of the wood **11**, turn right over a stile next to a gate into a field.

Follow the Sandy Rhine along the right hand edge of the field until you reach a horse gate on the bank to the right of a field gate.

Follow the green lane past a wood to a gate onto a road.

On the road, turn left and then right at the next junction. **12**

Follow the road for about a mile into Tockington village. **13**

Turn left to find the pub (The Swan).

FROM THE ALMONDSBURY SWAN TO TOCKINGTON

From the Swan **A**, cross the dual carriageway to the right hand side of the road opposite.

You need to take the path on the right, which descends through the trees just past the bus stop, but it is well worth making a detour to the car parking spaces fifty metres further on, which command a splendid view of the bridges over the Severn Estuary.

When the path emerges at a crossroads, go straight ahead along the dotted line to a path between two stone gate posts, which goes past the parish church.

The parish was once much bigger, stretching all the way down to the Full Moon pub in Stokes Croft. Over the centuries, pieces have been cut away, first Horfield and Filton, then Patchway and Bradley Stoke. The church remains an imposing edifice.

The path comes out beside the Bowl Inn on the far side of the churchyard **B**.

Turn left and proceed to a junction and then turn right down the main street.

Go past a junction on the left and a crossroads; then, when the road bends to the right, go straight ahead to a stile next to a gate at the top of a farm track. At the bottom of the hill, **B1** look for a stile on the right as the track bends to the left.

Follow the right hand hedge through three field boundaries, until you come to a double stile and bridge to the left of a gate into the field ahead.

Bear slightly left across the field to a stile next to a gate onto Moor Lane. **B2**

Turn right and follow the Lane under the motorway.

Turn left at the junction with Tockington Lane.

When the lane bends to the left at the edge of the village, cross the road to a path on the right 14, which goes down a drive to the fields beyond. (Or keep straight on along the road if you want to visit the Swan **13**.)

FROM THE SWAN INN AT TOCKINGTON TO HORTHAM WOOD

Retrace your steps and carry on past the junction on the right; then, when the road bends to the right, go straight on down a drive and climb a stile into a field. **14**

Follow the track down the middle of the field to the opposite hedge. Turn left and look for a gate on your right.

Go straight up through the next field and through a gate ahead. Follow the right hand hedge to the top of the hill, where there is an enclosed path that emerges on the A38. **15**

You may notice a campfire site on your right, which belongs to Woodhouse Park, the County Training, Activity and Camping Centre of Avon Scouts.

Cross the A38 with care and turn right and then left down Woodhouse Down. At the end of the road, go straight ahead alongside Tockington Park Wood and into Hortham Wood.

At the end of the wood look for a ladder stile over a deer fence ahead. **16**

FROM THE SWAN AT ALMONDSBURY TO HORTHAM WOOD

From the Swan **A**, turn right up the lane across a green open space. Do not be tempted by the first turning on the right (Redhouse Lane). You need to take the second turning, known as The Hill. Do not be put off by the appearance of this lane, which feels like a private drive. If you keep straight on, you will come to a kissing gate into a field.

Follow the path along the right hand edge of the field to another kissing gate into a residential road.

Go straight ahead across a cross road to a gate into another field.

Follow the path along the left hand hedge to find a stile into an enclosed path half-hidden in the corner.

Follow this path through a tunnel under the motorway **A1** to emerge over another stile into a field, which is sometimes filled with inquisitive horses in the summer.

There is a stile onto the road in the diagonally opposite corner.

In the lane, turn right and follow it until it rises over a bridge across the motorway. Just before the motorway **A2**, look for a path down the slope to a stile on the left. Over the stile, follow the right hand hedge past a pool formed by the confluence of two drains and enter the path through Hortham Wood opposite.

At the end of the wood, turn right and look for a ladder stile over a deer fence ahead **16.**

FROM HORTHAM WOOD TO THE LEISURE CENTRE

Over the stile **16**, turn left and cross a bridge over a brook. The bridge looks broken, but it seems to be strong enough!

Over the bridge, turn left along the ride between the hedge and a new plantation and carry on until you reach another ladder stile.

The next section is often overgrown with nettles and brambles, which makes this route most suitable for the winter or early spring.

Just after the path crosses a wooden bridge with a stile at either end, use the footbridge **17** over the motorway on your right. *(The wooden bridge is sometimes under water in the winter, but it seems quite sound!)*

Over the stile at the bottom of the steps on the other side of the footbridge, go straight ahead, following the hedge on your left, until you have crossed another three stiles.

After the third stile, follow the hedge on your right, until you emerge through an electric fence onto a farm drive. The fence onto the drive is equipped with a handle for disconnecting it, but there is no such device after the third stile, so you will need to take care.

Turn right on the drive which will take you onto a road, where you will find a horse gate **18** straight ahead, leading into a bridle path through an avenue of trees. This path was very wet underfoot in January, but the going was firm underneath.

At the end of the wood, the path goes through another hunting gate into an enclosed ride, at the end of which is a spinney with a bridge and another hunting gate on your right. Through the gate, turn left along the bridle path until the next field boundary, after which there is another hunting gate on your right. This represents a diversion of the bridle path from the route on the OS map caused by the development of Green Farm in Gaunt's Earthcott.

Through the gate, make for a similar gate in the diagonally opposite corner of the field.

Through this gate, turn right to find another gate, through which you should bear left to find an exit from the field in the hedge ahead.

Turn sharp left to find a gate, a stile and a plank bridge onto the road.

Turn left past the entrance to Green Farm to find a stile into the field on your right. (This is also not in the place indicated on the OS map.) **19**

In the field, bear left to a stile near some farm buildings.

In the next field, the right of way hugs the left hand edge around the corner and along the far side to a bridge protected by a pair of stiles onto a metalled farm track. **20**

Turn left and follow the track until it bends sharply to the left.

Turn right immediately after the bend and go straight ahead through a gap into the next field. (It was partially blocked by a fallen tree in January 2007.)

Bear right across the field to find the bridge over Hortham Brook into the Woodlands Golf Course. **21**

Over the bridge, which is protected by two stiles, turn left on the permissive path alongside the brook. (Brambles can be a hazard along this stretch.)

When the path emerges into the open, turn right toward a barn like structure.

The path goes in front of the barn to connect with a metalled drive.

Turn left on the drive, which passes the club house, and make your way onto the road. (You may have to climb a couple of stiles if the gates are shut.) **22**

The Club House

Turn right on the road, which crosses over the motorway to a roundabout. Turn left at this roundabout and also at the next one. **23**

Carry on down Ormond's Close until the last turning on the right before the end.

Carry on to a bridge over Patchway Brook and turn right.

Bear left at the first opportunity along the track that leads back to the Leisure Centre.

If you feel that you deserve some alcoholic refreshment at the finish, the Three Brooks, which is at the next roundabout from the leisure centre, is a good bet.

5: BEYOND BRADLEY STOKE
OR 'THE SAGE' - rather further than a half-marathon
From the Club House at Woodlands Golf Course ST625829

This route begins at the Club House of Woodlands Golf Course, which is just over the M4 from Bradley Stoke. It could just as easily have started at the Leisure Centre, at the White Horse in Hambrook or at the Globe in Frampton Cotterell, and there is a lot to be said for starting out from Parkway Railway Station, but for a route entitled 'Beyond Bradley Stoke' only Woodlands club house will really do.

The map of the route resembles Yoda from Star Wars, which is why the route is subtitled 'The Sage', although, to be honest, he looks more like a cross between Baldrick in Blackadder and a terrier bitch that used to belong to my brother.

The Tao Te Ching has this to say of the sages of old:

> *The ancient masters were subtle, mysterious, profound, responsive.*
> *The depth of their knowledge is unfathomable.*
> *Because it is unfathomable,*
> *All we can do is describe their appearance:*
> *Watchful, like men crossing a winter stream*
> *Alert, like men aware of danger*

Courteous, like visiting guests
Yielding, like ice about to melt
Simple, like uncarved blocks of wood
Hollow, like caves
Opaque, like muddy pools.

The line 'Courteous like visiting guests' should remind those, who park in the ample golf course car park, to tell the management what you are doing and to spend some money in the club house bar, which is open to all, when you have finished the route.

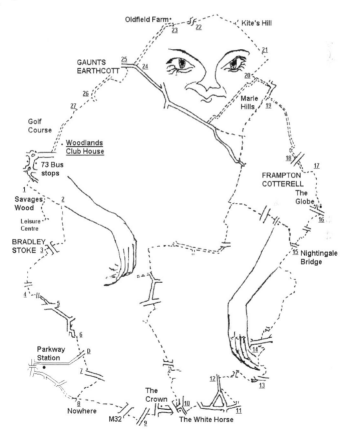

As another passage in the Tao Te Ching has it: "The highest good is like water," so it is appropriate that a route subtitled the sage should follow many streams: first the Patchway Brook, then Hortham Brook, Stoke Brook and the Ham Brook. After crossing the Bradley Brook, it follows The Frome Valley Walkway alongside the river to the edge of Iron Acton before it climbs over the ridge of the Marle Hills and Kite's Hill to Gaunts Earthcott and a return along the Hortham Brook.

However, we should also remember the lines:

> *'Watchful, like men crossing a winter stream*
> *Alert, like men aware of danger,'*

because the River Frome is apt to overflow its banks after heavy rain, when it is necessary to exercise extreme caution. If you have parked at the golf course, you should remember to be a 'courteous guest'; but refreshments are also available en route in Hambrook, where the White Horse has currently got the highest on-line rating, or at the Globe in Frampton Cotterell.

Some other possibilities are available to those who use public transport. The 73, 73A and 73B buses stop between the two roundabouts at the beginning of the route. They also stop at Parkway Railway Station, from which a spur joins the main route at 'Nowhere'. On the way back, you might like to visit the Three Brooks or the Parkway Tavern before you catch your bus. Also the 483 from Yate to Cribbs Causeway stops near the Leisure Centre and also at Frampton Cotterell Church next to the Globe, opening up the possibility of doing half the route at a time, if you get the timing right.

Seasonal Hazards: Flooding alongside the River Frome
Brambles going into Woodlands golf course

FROM WOODLANDS GOLF CLUB TO HAMBROOK
(about 4 miles)

If you have parked in the car park, make your way back to the road and turn right over the motorway bridge to a roundabout and turn left down Bowsland.

This is where the 73, 73A and 73B buses put down, one stop before the Trench Lane/Bowsland Way stop.

At the next roundabout, go straight ahead down Ellick's Close.

Go down the second cul-de-sac on the right, which leads to a bridge over the Patchway Brook.

Over the bridge, turn left into Savage's Wood. **1**

Make your way through the wood, keeping nearly parallel with the brook to a stile and kissing gate.

Keep going on a cinder track alongside Patchway Brook. This joins the Hortham Brook, which approaches unseen through a culvert under the motorway behind some bushes on the left, as the track bends to the right. Carry on until you reach the Three Brooks Lake. **2**

This lake was formed by damming the Bradley Brook, which is formed by the confluence of Hortham Brook and Stoke Brook.

By the lake, turn right, keeping Stoke Brook on your left until it passes under a road-bridge overhead.

On the far side of the bridge, turn left over the brook **3** and then right along a muddy woodland path, with the stream on your right.

Keep going through the wood (Sherbourne's Brake) until you cross Bailey's Court Road beside a roundabout.

After about100m, turn left down a path between some houses. **4**

Cross one road and turn right at a junction to emerge at some pedestrian traffic lights on Winterbourne Road. **5**

Over the road, carry on, on same line up Mead Road to a junction.

Turn right down North Road and left down Rocks Lane, which

is the second on the left and is marked by a blue signpost to Parkway etc.

Before Rocks Lane bends to the right, turn left and then right on a cycle path signed to Parkway and the University of the West of England. **6**

Go straight on over Hunt's Ground Road, **(D)** following signs to the University of West of England, **[Turn right and follow signs to Parkway Station if that is how you arrived.]** until you emerge over a railway bridge onto a road. **7**

Turn left down the road, to find a kissing gate on the right.

In the field, go straight on to another kissing gate.

Some new planting and fencing has confused matters here, and the line of the new hedge directs you to a kissing gate and a bridge over Ham Brook. Do not be led astray. You need to turn left at this point. **8**

The new planting marks 'Nowhere', because, according the Stoke Gifford parish walk leaflet, this patch was left off parish maps. This is also the best point to join the route if you came by train to Parkway Railway Station.

[Turn left out of the station and then left again under a railway bridge. Go straight ahead at the first mini roundabout. Then turn right and immediately left down a track at the next junction. Go straight on at the end of the track to a metal stile and join the main route. 8]

Continue alongside Ham Brook to a kissing gate.

Through the gate, carry on in the same direction to another kissing gate.

Keep going along the hedge on your right to a muddy corner, where you must turn right over a stile onto an enclosed path under the motorway.

Through the tunnel, climb a stile into a path alongside Ham Brook, which emerges on Old Gloucester Road. **9**

(It is possible to follow the brook to its confluence with the Frome, if you do not wish to visit the pub. See **the Duchess** in Vol. 1.)

Turn left up the Old Gloucester Road and look for a footpath on the right (after about. 200m).

In the road, turn left and then right past **The Crown Inn** (rated 5.5/10 on **www.beerintheevening.co.uk**) and under the motorway.

Check out some shorter routes from Hambroook and Frampton Cotterell available free at www.closertothecountryside.co.uk).

The White Horse

FROM HAMBROOK TO THE GLOBE (about 3.5 miles)

After crossing the Bradley Brook, turn right down Mill Lane past the **White Horse**(6.5/10) **10** and the **Hambrook** (4.0/10) which includes a Chinese restaurant.

Take the first footpath on the left alongside the Frome (*just before the lane crosses the Bradley Brook. The confluence with the Frome is usually out of sight).*

At the end of the path, turn right on the road across the river. Take care as there is a blind bend.

Follow the river on your left.

Ignore the first turning on your left, which follows the River Frome Walkway (although it is a viable shortcut) and the second.

Take the third turning on the left down an apparent drive, and look for a stone stile on the left. **11**

This leads into Bury Hill Fort a Neolithic fort, allegedly modified by the Romans. In wet weather, you may find that it has been more obviously modified by horses.

There is another stone stile in the diagonally opposite corner of the fort, which leads to a steep descent to the road and the Frome Valley Walkway.

Turn right alongside the river just before the road crosses a bridge. **12**

Follow the track alongside the river, through a new kissing gate and an older one until you reach a footbridge over the river.

Over the river turn right along a substantial path, which emerges, past a garage, into 'The Dingle'.

Go straight ahead to a T-junction and then turn right over the river.

Turn left through a kissing gate on the other side and follow the enclosed path alongside the river. **13**

Be "watchful, like a man crossing a winter stream", if the river is high!

The Forest Path veers off to the right just before a stile, which blocks the path close to the railway viaduct. Climb this stile and another and cross the footbridge. **14**

To the left is a kissing gate into the Huckford Quarry Nature Reserve ("Hollow, like a cave"). The pennant sandstone from the quarry provided the core of the viaduct, which is faced in brick. The conditions in the quarry are more acidic than the surrounding countryside, which means that the stunted oaks to be found there are more common in Wales than they are in the lowlands of England. A leaflet describing the site mentions three types of fern, polypody, lady fern and hart's tongue fern and some attractive wildflowers growing around the quarry, including stitchwort, bluebells, violets, foxgloves, Yellow Archangel and Wood Anemone. Wild Strawberries can also be found.

Turn right and follow the path under the viaduct. Do not be seduced into climbing the path up the hill, the correct route is straight on to a stile into a field and a path that leads to a pair of stiles onto a track that leads to a bridge back to the other side of the river.

Turn left to follow the path alongside the river.

In January 2007, the path was under water at this point, as it was at several other points. Here, it was possible ("Alert, like men aware of danger") to get round the problem by diverting up the bank into the field.

A kissing gate leads to a long damp meadow beside the river and another kissing gate leading into the scrubby forerunner of a wood.

The barrier into the wood has been removed.

When we went through, two cock pheasants rose up. This was not an accident; there is a pheasant feeder in the wood. "Opaque, like a muddy pool", the path was also flooded in the wood, which necessitated a paddle, since there was no way around.

There is a kissing gate out of the wood.

The next kissing gate showed a thigh-high tide mark, so we remained *"alert, like men aware of danger"*.

There is no right of way across the bridge on the left, which is not marked on my map.

You need to go though a kissing gate next to the track that leads away from the bridge and then through another onto a track on the far side of the field.

This is the track to Nightingale's Bridge.**15**

Go straight ahead through a kissing gate and look for another kissing gate on the left.

Follow the enclosed path alongside the river (which can also get dangerously flooded) until you get to a bridge and a pair of gates into a field.

Follow the path around a garden graced with a large model railway to emerge through a pair of kissing gates onto a road.

Turn left over Parsonage Bridge and then turn right to follow the river through a grassy area to emerge onto a road.

Turn left towards the Parish Church and the Globe Inn **16**

FROM FRAMPTON COTTERELL TO BRADLEY STOKE (c.5.5 M)

Turn right down Mill Lane between the Globe Inn and the Parish Church

Follow the lane past some houses to a stile next to a barrier protecting a steelyard.

Go through the yard to find a kissing gate at the end on the right. Follow the enclosed path, which emerges through a gap beside a stile into a field.

Go straight ahead to another gap and follow the river until the path disappears into the trees. **17**

Keep left and follow the boundary between the field and a rough area, which is marked as a wood on the map.

When you reach a hedge corner, turn right to find a gate into an enclosed track to the B4058. Remain *"alert, like men aware of danger"*. **18**

Cross over into a green lane, called Cogmill Lane and follow it for a long kilometre to a junction with a metalled road near Southview Farm. **19**

Turn right and follow the road around a bend to the left and another to the right and then turn immediately left down a bridle path or farm track.

When the track bends sharply to the left, go straight ahead over a padlocked gate near a barn. (The OS map is inaccurate at this point.) **20**

Past the barn area, turn right through a gap in the hedge and go straight ahead across the field to a kink in the hedge on the far side. (A hedge, marked on the OS map, has been grubbed up, but there was a pair of tractor tyre tracks across the field when I reccied the route.)

Climb the stile into the next field, which is concealed around a corner.

Make for a stile next to a field gate in the left hand side of the field. **21**

Over this stile, follow the right hand hedge to a double stile and bridge in the far right hand corner of the field.

Go straight ahead up the hill to another pair of stiles over a bridge and on up to a single stile at the top of the ridge.

This is Kites Hill. I did not see a kite, but I did see a pair of ravens and a buzzard.

The stile at the far side of the field is about twenty metres from the corner of the field.

Keep going straight ahead, parallel to the left hand hedge to a stile behind a willow tree, which marks the site of an old pond. Bear left to find a stile next to a gate near an oak tree. This is a large, complex field, which must have been formed by grubbing up several hedges. At the time of writing, half was down to grass and half appeared to be down to maize. It is probably best to head for the first corner on the left of the hedge opposite and work your way left along the hedge until you find the gate.

Once over the stile, go straight ahead to a stile onto the B4427, which is a bit of a rat run. **22**

The right of way on the other side of the road uses a stile in the hedge. But it was overgrown and I did not see it until I went over the gate to the left and looked back.

The right of way then goes more or less straight across the field to a double stile and bridge into a series of horse paddocks. However, there was an electric cattle fence across the middle of the field, and the paddocks were also divided by electric fences, so I decided to use the gate on the left, which led onto a concrete farm track around Oldfield Farm. (If you wish to follow the right of way precisely, it goes diagonally left across the horse paddocks, through a couple of electric fences to a gate onto the concrete track.) **23**

The right of way from Oldfield Farm to Gaunts Earthcott zigzags across the fields, presumably following field boundaries that no longer exist. You will probably prefer to follow the farm track, which goes in a straight line from a bridle gate into the yard of Oldfield Farm down an enclosed track and across another field, under a power line to emerge over a pair of field gates onto a minor road. **24**

Turn right to find a stile into the field on your left past Court Farm - this path is not in the place indicated on the OS map. **25**
In the field, bear left to a stile near some farm buildings.

In the next field, the right of way hugs the left hand edge around the corner and along the far side to a bridge protected by a pair of stiles onto a metalled farm track.

Turn left and follow the track until it bends sharply to the left. **26**
Turn right immediately after the bend and go straight ahead through a gap into the next field. (It was partially blocked by a fallen tree in January 2007.)

Bear right across the field to find the bridge over Hortham Brook into the Woodlands Golf Course. **27**

Over the bridge, which is protected by two stiles, turn left on the permissive path alongside the brook. (Brambles can be a hazard along this stretch.)

When the path emerges into the open, turn right towards a barn like structure.

The path goes in front of the barn to connect with a metalled drive.

Turn left on the drive, which passes the club house on your left.

If this is where you have parked your car, do not forget to be a 'courteous guest!'

If you started somewhere else, return to the beginning of the chapter to find your way back.

6: AROUND COALPIT HEATH

WITH GENERAL de GAULLE 9 miles (approx)

From the Globe Inn in Frampton Cotterell - ST667820

This route starts from the Globe Inn a popular pub, specialising in food, which also has well kept beer including Courage, Bass, Doom Bar, Butcombe and a couple of guests, which vary from day to day. There are also three varieties of cider including Black Rat in the fridge out the back. It will be interesting to see how it competes with the new Bath Ales pub, the Live and Let Live, which has recently opened in the village.

The name of the pub introduces an international dimension. This is partly because it invites us to consider the whole world, but also because the image of General de Gaulle has mysteriously emerged in the map of the route.

This is not inappropriate, because the route passes among the fragmentary remains of South Gloucestershire's coal and steel industries. The Roden Acre iron mine used to be in the field behind the church, linked by a Dramway to Iron Acton. A later part of the route passes between the remains of some of the coal mines of Coalpit Heath.

The image of the general reminds us that coal and steel used to be the basis of wealth and politics, and the European Coal and Steel Community (ECSC) was the forerunner of the European Economic Community (EEC), now the European Community (EC) one of the Three Pillars of the European Union (EU).

The Tao Te Ching has been used by economists (following Hayek) and right wing politicians to attack institutions like the EU, selectively deploying extracts from passages such as:

> *The more laws and restrictions there are,*
> *The poorer people become.*
> *The sharper men's weapons,*
> *The more trouble in the land.*
> *The more ingenious and clever men are,*
> *The more strange things happen.*
> *The more rules and regulations,*
> *The more thieves and robbers.*

It is not difficult to guess which parts get left out! In addition, there are other passages in the Tao Te Ching, which point in a different direction as we shall see.

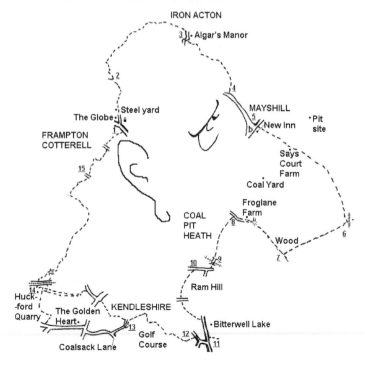

If you are walking this route after heavy rain, you would do well to remember the following passage:

> *Under heaven, nothing is more soft and yielding than water.*
> *Yet for attacking the solid and strong, nothing is better.*
> *It has no equal.*

The Frome takes its name from an ancient British name meaning a torrent, which helps to explain the many devices along its length, which are designed to regulate its flow. The path alongside the river is often flooded and, when it is, you must be prepared to take the occasional detour to avoid being swept away.

Food can be had en route at the New Inn in Mayshill and the Golden Heart in Kendleshire as well as on your return to the Globe Inn.

If you are travelling by bus, the 483 between Cribbs Causeway and Yate stops beside the pub.

Seasonal Hazards: Flooding alongside the Frome River
Inquisitive heifers past Says Court Farm
Golf balls on golf course

FROM THE GLOBE TO THE NEW INN

Turn left and go down Mill Lane between the Globe Inn **1** and the Parish Church.

The footpath off to the right leads to the site of the old iron workings at the Roden Acre Mine, which used to be linked to Iron Acton by a dramway.

Follow the lane past some houses to a stile next to a barrier protecting a **steel-holding yard**.

(The footpath off to the left leads to the Centenary Field, which contains half a large pithead wheel, commemorating the Roden Acre Mine and nineteenth century iron--miners from Frampton Cotterell.)

Go through the yard to find a kissing gate at the end on the right.

Follow the enclosed path, which emerges through a gap beside a stile into a field. *This path is quite narrow and nettles can be a problem. It is possible to get round this by taking a detour through the Centenary field, but the gap through the hedge in the right hand corner is not a right of way so it may get blocked if the farmer needs to put stock in the next field.*

Go straight ahead and follow the river as the path disappears into the trees. **2** *The first gap leads to a path that is often flooded, but the path through the second gap is drier.*

Cross the river by a footbridge and turn left to follow the river on the other bank.

You will pass the Ladden Brook confluence on the left. This stream, which rises in the Parish of Tytherington adds considerably to the volume of water in the Frome.

Follow the narrower Frome upstream under two power cables and over three stiles (one hidden beside a barn) until you reach a ford across the river.

The ford , which carries Hover's Lane from Frampton End to the Bristol Road, was flooded the last time I was there, making it uncomfortable to use the stiles on either side of the track. Luckily, there is also a convenient pair of gates.

In any case, keep on the same bank until you come to a pair of stiles at either end of an enclosed path leading to a patch of rough vegetation, including nettles and hemlock.

At the other end of the rough patch, another pair of stiles leads up the embankment of the old mineral railway from the Roden Acre Mine.

Cross the river on the track of the old railway and turn right along the other bank beside an extensive lawn and then through some rougher vegetation, until you emerge on the road from Iron Acton at Algars Court. **3**

Turn right past a stone barn, a red cliff, Algar's Mill (*mentioned in Doomsday Book*) and Algar's Manor and then turn left on the Frome Walkway.

The Walkway goes through the Algar's Manor nature reserve trail, where I saw a buzzard being mobbed by crows, to Tubbs Bottom Detention Reservoir.

I do not know exactly what this does, but after heavy rain it involves a lot of furious rushing and gurgling. I suspect there is an underground reservoir connected with old mine workings. Notices proclaim that these are dangerous waters and they certainly look it! The Algar's Manor nature trail continues through the wood on the other side, but our route continues straight ahead.

Go over one stile and past Tubbs Bottom Farm Bridge, named by a sign affixed by the Environment Agency.

Follow the path away from the river to a gate, through which you need to look for a stile on the right just before a hedge corner.

Follow the left hand hedge until you emerge via a track onto a minor road. **4**

Turn left on the road and follow it through the hamlet of Mayshill past two greens (keep left at the second) until it emerges on the A432 opposite the New Inn. **5**

FROM MAYSHILL TO HENFIELD

On the left hand side of the pub, follow the metalled drive to Says Court Farm.

You can see an industrial site off to the right, which is appropriate, because there is a disused Pit Shaft 500m to the northeast and a Coal Yard on the site of Froglane Colliery 500m to the southwest.

Negotiate the right of way around the left hand side of the farm along a track consisting mainly of rubble.

At the end, you need to get onto a track, which was wired off the last time I was there. It is not too difficult to climb through.

Turn left and look for a gate on your right after you have gone under a power line.

Through the gate, bear left down the field, under another power line to a stile in the far corner of the field.

Go straight ahead to a gate into the next field (not the gate on the left).

Keep going along a tractor track across the field to a bridge across the ditch on the left. (The flat stones of the bridge were on the far bank the last time I was there, but it was easy enough to step over the ditch.)

Turn right alongside the ditch and follow the power line until it crosses the railway line on your left.

This is a branch-line leading to the Murco oil terminal at Westerleigh Railhead. This is owned by the Murphy Oil Corporation of Arkansas, which also owns a tanker terminal at Grays in Essex and another at Milford Haven. I saw a long train of Murco tanker wagons coming away from the terminal hauled by an engine bearing the markings 60020 EW&S, if that means anything to you train spotters out there! (EW&S stands for English Welsh and Scottish.)

Do not go under the line, but turn right over a stile, and keep right alongside a hedge to a footbridge over a stream.

Keep straight on up the hill with a hedge on your left to look for a stile on your left.

Over the stile, keep straight on with a hedge on your right to another footbridge half way along the far hedge.

Go straight ahead under a power line to the corner of a wood.

Keep straight ahead with the wood on your right to a pair of stiles through the corner of the wood. 7

Turn right alongside the wood.

Keep going with a hedge on your right and the main railway to London on your left until you emerge over a gate onto a lane.

This is Frog Lane. Frog Lane Coal Yard (formerly Colliery) is a few hundred metres to the right. To the left is the track of a disused branch line, which used to pass under the main line between Parkway and London to join the colliery to the Murco branch near the abattoir south of Kidney Hill. It is presumably also the line of one branch of the original Dramway down to the River Avon.

Go straight ahead over a metal fence next to a gate and carry on through the yard of Froglane Farm *(where they were power hosing a traction engine when I reccied the route)* to emerge on a road.

Keep going until you come to a stile on the left. **8**

Follow the right hand hedge around the edge of the field until you come to a stile in the hedge ahead.

Go straight ahead to a pair of kissing gates onto a footbridge over the main line from Parkway to London and Gloucester. *You are now on the beginning of the Dramway footpath.* **9**

When you emerge on a road, turn right.

Go straight ahead past the first junction to find a track on the left. **10**

Follow the Dramway past one kissing gate and through another to emerge on a lane past a cricket club.

Cross the lane to a stile into a field.

Go straight on to another stile and then on to a metal stile into a stable yard and a gap onto a road.

In the road, turn right and go past Bitterwell Lake *(once used to soak pit props, but now a carp lake).*

Go straight on past a Dramway sign pointing into a field on the left to a road junction. **11**

FROM HENFIELD TO HUCKFORD QUARRY *(On the Forest Path)*

Turn right at the junction.

Keep going past the first junction on the left and look for a stile onto a golf course on the left. **12**

On the golf course, follow the drive to the car parks.

Turn right, through the first car park to find a cinder track, which follows the edge of the course to the Half Way Halt café.

Keep on the track as it bends to the right to a field gate.

Turn left just before the gate and follow the path alongside the road past two gates to a kissing gate onto Ruffet Road. **13**

To visit the GOLDEN HEART

If you wish to visit the Golden Heart, turn left to the junction with Coalsack Lane.

Turn right and proceed to the junction with Badminton Road (the A432). Cross the road with care, and turn right and then left down the road opposite.

The Golden Heart is on your right. (It is particularly welcoming in those seasons when the fire is lit.)

This is a suitable place to consider the following passage from the Tao:
I have three treasures, which I hold and keep
The first is mercy; the second is economy;
The third is daring not to be ahead of others.
From mercy comes courage; from economy comes generosity;
From humility comes leadership.
Nowadays men shun mercy, but try to be brave;
They abandon economy, but try to be generous;
They do not believe in humility, but always try to be first;
This is certain death.

When you emerge, carry on down the hill to Damsons Bridge.

Just before the bridge, turn right on the path along the River Frome Walkway. **14**

Otherwise:

On the road, turn right to find a gate onto the section of the golf course on the left.

Pass to the right of the first lake, then cross a stone bridge to pass the second lake on the left.

Keep going until you find a sleeper bridge over a ditch near a field boundary.

Over this bridge, follow way-marks on white-painted logs across the golf course to stile onto a lay-by on the A430.

Turn left in the lay-by to find a safe crossing over the main road. (Watch out for traffic turning into Park Road.) Continue along the pavement up Park Road to find a footpath along the drive of Ivory House on the left.

The path descends through the wood on to a metalled lane.

In the lane, turn right and continue across a new junction to the end of the lane.

It was at this junction that we once found a group of benighted youths who had gone exploring up the River Frome and had lost their way. We sent them to Badminton Road to find their way home to Downend. The junction itself is an oddity. It seems to have something to do with maintenance work on the railway to the right.

At the end of the lane, turn left over the stile and descend to the river near the viaduct.

Turn right over a stile to leave the Forest Path.

[Here the two routes recombine.]

Follow the River Frome Walkway over a bridge across the river. **14**

We have already encountered this stretch of the Frome Walkway in the previous chapter. A free leaflet can be obtained from libraries and other council premises, or you can download a copy on the internet.

FROM THE QUARRY TO THE GLOBE

To the left is a kissing gate into the Huckford Quarry Nature Reserve. The pennant sandstone from the quarry provided the core of the viaduct, which is faced in brick. The conditions in the quarry are more acidic than the surrounding countryside, so it contains some plants that are unusual in this area, such as the sort of oak tree that is more commonly seen forming low scrub on Welsh hillsides.

Turn right and follow the path under the viaduct. Do not be seduced into climbing the path up the hill, the correct route is straight on to a stile into a field and a path that leads to a pair of stiles onto a track that leads to a bridge back to the other side of the river.

Turn left to follow the path alongside the river.

In January 2007, the path was under water at this point, as it was at several other points. Here, it was possible to get round the problem by diverting up the bank into the field. (NB it was even worse at the end of June the same year!)

A kissing gate leads to a long damp meadow beside the river and another kissing gate leading into the scrubby forerunner of a wood.

The barrier into the wood has been removed.

When we went through, two cock pheasants rose up. This was not an accident; there is a pheasant feeder in the wood. The path was also flooded in the wood, which necessitated a paddle, since there was no way around.

There is a kissing gate out of the wood.

The next kissing gate showed a thigh-high tide mark.

There is no right of way across the bridge on the left, which is not marked on my map.

You need to go though a kissing gate next to the track that leads away from the bridge and then through another onto a track on the far side of the field.

This is the track to Nightingale's Bridge. **15**

Go straight ahead through a kissing gate and look for another kissing gate on the left.

Follow the enclosed path alongside the river until you get to a bridge and a pair of gates into a field. *This section also floods from time to time.*

Follow the path around a garden graced with a large model railway to emerge through a pair of kissing gates onto a road. Turn left over Parsonage Bridge and then turn right to follow the river through a grassy area to emerge onto a road.

When the path emerges onto a road, turn left to return to the Globe.

7: COAL AND COUNTRY
OR 'NON!' - nearly 10 miles
From the Old Inn in Westerleigh -ST 699796

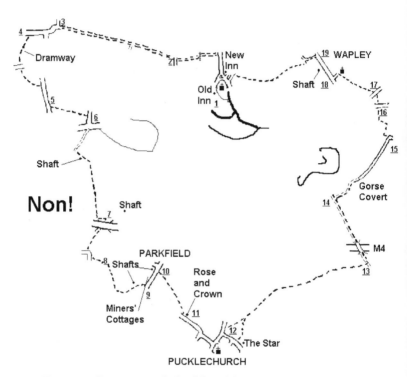

You can live your whole life without seeing the face of General de Gaulle in a map. Then all of a sudden he turns up twice in three days. It must be the antibiotics!

General de Gaulle famously refused to allow the United Kingdom, under Harold Macmillan to join the Common Market (or EEC) as it was then known. He was anxious about the UK's links with the US and the Commonwealth. But he might have had a different attitude if he had read the Tao Te Ching:

If a great country gives way to a smaller country,
It will conquer the smaller country.
And if a small country submits to a great country,
It will conquer the great country.
Therefore those who would conquer must yield,
And those who conquer do so because they yield.
A great country needs more people;
A small country needs to serve.
Each gets what it wants.
It is fitting for a great nation to yield.

This loop, connecting the Forest Path to the old mining communities of Westerleigh, Pucklechurch and Wapley, sums up this section of the book. It only adds one Gorse Covert to the sum of forestal connections, but it serves to demonstrate the rural nature of the South Gloucestershire coalfield as it passes several disused coal shafts en route. There are also opportunities for train spotters and connoisseurs of rural churches.

The Old Inn at Westerleigh (especially valued on account of its rough cider) and the Rose and Crown at Pucklechurch are well worth a visit, as is the Star, which features in the next route.
There is no bus service to Westerleigh, from Bristol, as far as I can tell, although Ebley Coaches run a service (620)

between Bath and Tetbury that calls there. However, you can access the route in Pucklechurch, if you use the 689 service between Bristol and Yate.

Known Hazards: Mineral railway in Westerleigh

FROM WESTERLEIGH TO THE ROSE AND CROWN (c. 5 miles)

From the Old Inn **1** turn right and then left at the junction past the church.

Go down the main-street to find a track towards the end on the left.

Go down the track over a railway line to a junction in the track. **2**

Go straight on down Broad Lane for about a mile (1600m), ignoring the first turning to the left after 1000m, until you emerge on a metalled lane. **3**

On the road, go straight ahead past a road junction on the left to find a track on the left. **4**

This is the beginning of the Dramway footpath.

Follow the Dramway past one kissing gate and through another to emerge on a lane past a cricket club.

Cross the lane to a stile into a field.

Go straight on to another stile and then on to a metal stile into a stable yard and a gap onto a road.

In the road, turn right, go past Bitterwell Lake and look for a kissing gate on the left. **5**

Bitterwell Lake was once used to soak pit props, but now stocks carp.

In the field, follow the Dramway Path through one rough gate, a kissing gate and a horse gate onto a road past a cottage.

In the road, turn right toward a major rat run. **6**

Cross this road with care to a gap beside a field gate into a bridle path.

Follow the bridle path to a sign-posted kissing gate on the left opposite a horse exercising machine in a farmyard.

In field, bear right past a scrubby hummock in the middle of the field to a barb-wired field gate in the diagonally opposite corner.

The scrub conceals the disused mineshaft of Parkgate Colliery.

Over the wired gate, go straight ahead keeping a hedge on your left.

This gate was open the last time I went there, and a roe deer fled from behind the hedge.

Go through an empty gateway, and keep going straight on until you reach a double stile and bridge.

Over the stiles, go straight ahead to a kissing gate and then bear left to find the tunnel under the motorway (M4). **7**

In the tunnel, the small gate to the right of a field gate has a shin catcher. If the middle gates are shut there are steps to the right. Through the tunnel, go straight ahead along the track past Lyde Green Farm.

This track is something of a highway because it was used to move the slagheap, which used to be more evident, on the left. It is still possible to make out the irreducible rump of the slagheap, which used to belong to Parkfield Colliery on the escarpment above. The chimney of the colliery is still visible from this point. It used to be more of a landmark on the M4, but it is becoming hidden by trees.

On the road, turn left through a kissing gate into a horse field. In the field, keep the hedge on your left to find a kissing gate onto a disused railway path. **8**

This is the line of the actual Dramway. The Murco terminal is on the continuation of the track bed on the other side of the motorway. However, this is also where we leave the Dramway footpath.

Go straight ahead over a stile and through a kissing gate into a field.

In the field bear right, keeping to the left of a spur.

Carry on through a deep muddy patch into a wood and look for a stile on the left.

Over this stile, turn right to another stile, a bridge and yet another stile on the left into a field.

In the field, bear right up the steep slope to a stile and then keep going up to another stile between two piles of rubble.

Carry on over the stile to a coal pit tump, and then turn right along a farm track to a gate onto the road. **9**

Turn left past 'The Rank', *a row of miners' cottages built by coal-owner, Handel Cossham, who also built Cossham Hospital in Kingswood.*

At the end of the cottages, turn right over a stile beside a gate into a field. **10**

Just beyond the cottages is another disused pit, disguised as a children's playground. There is another on the other side of the motorway. This was all part of the Parkfield Colliery.

In the field, follow the left hand hedge until it swings off to the left.

Carry straight on across the field to the diagonally opposite corner, where there is a stile onto a road (Parkfield Road).

Turn left to the Rose and Crown. **11**

FROM THE ROSE AND CROWN TO WESTERLEIGH (c.4.5 miles)

From the pub, turn left down Parkfield Road towards the village Church.

In the main road, turn left and go past a junction with a sign to Pucklechurch Primary School.

The house on the corner is the Old School House.

After the Old School House, look for an enclosed path on the right, which leads past the school field. **12**

In the next field, go straight ahead down the middle of the field to a double stile and bridge over Feltham Brook at the far end. (There is sometimes a wire fence across this field that requires a diversion.)

Over the bridge, turn left, with the brook on your left and turn right as the brook turns you towards a hedge corner to the right. (Field boundaries on the map have been grubbed up on this farm.)

Over the stile to the left of the hedge corner, go straight on, with the hedge on your right to a stile near some farm buildings.

Over the stile, bear left across a large field to a bridge over a ditch. (Aim just to the right of the third wooden power pole from the motorway.)

Over the bridge, go straight ahead up the field to a gate onto a track. **13**

Turn left over the motorway (M4).

Over the bridge, go straight on up Burbarrow Lane and take the first proper track on the right. **14**

When the track passes Gorse Covert, it is marked on the map as a 'road generally less than 4m wide', but that is something of an exaggeration.

Look for a stile on the left, about 500m past Gorse Covert. It is nearly at the top of the hill. **15**

Follow the path across one field to another stile.

Turn right and follow the hedge on the right to a stile onto a road. **16**

Cross the road to another stile into a field and cross that field to a wooden stile onto a road. **17**

Turn left and look for another stile on the right into a field.

In the field, bear leftish to a stile hidden behind a projecting section of the hedge ahead.

Over the stile follow the hedge on the left past a riding centre to another stile and some white gates beneath some horse chestnuts into Wapley Churchyard.

Go past the church into a drive and turn left to the road.
In the road turn right. **18**

There is a disused mineshaft in a field on the left opposite Church Farm but it is difficult to make out from the road.

Past Church Farm, look for a hunting gate beside a gate on your left **19** to follow the drive towards Wychwell Farm.

I saw two roe deer at this point when I checked out the route. One fled before I could operate the zoom on my camera. The second stood still and watched me, but the batteries had gone flat!

As the drive bends to the right, go straight on to a hunting gate, a bridge and a kissing gate into a field.

In the field, go straight ahead through to a gap in the hedge to the right of a farm (Beanwood Farm).

Go straight ahead to another gap, then diagonally right to a pair of hunting gates and a kissing gate onto a lane.

Turn left along the lane to a road, then turn right and then left around church to the Old Inn.

This country route through the remains of the old Gloucestershire coalfield reminds us that there other ways of life. It is written in the Tao Te Ching:

> *A small country has fewer people.*
> *Though there are machines that can work 10 to 100 times faster than man,*
> *they are not needed.*
> *The people take death seriously and do not travel far.*
> *Though they have boats and carriages, no one uses them.*
> *Though they have armour and weapons, no one displays them.*
> *Men return to knotting ropes in place of writing.*
> *Their food is plain and good, their clothes fine but simple,*
> *their homes secure.*
> *They are happy in their ways.*

Though they live within sight of their neighbours,
And crowing cocks and barking dogs are heard
across the way,
They leave each other in peace while they grow old
and die.

8: THE STAR
OR THE JANUS LION - 11miles (approx.)
From the Star at Pucklechurch -ST702766

It is written in the Tao Te Ching:
> *A brave and passionate man will kill or be killed.*
> *A brave and calm man will always preserve life.*
> *Of these two, which is good and which is harmful?*
> *Some things are not favoured by Heaven. Who knows why?*
> *Even the sage is unsure of this.*

The Star Inn is a particularly appropriate place to contemplate the sage's dilemma, because it was here, one night, that the landlord, Bob Todd, heard a disturbance on the green opposite the pub and went out to remonstrate with the trouble makers. He was knocked over and killed by the hooligans' car. Taoist sages usually take a quietist line, urging inaction. But the Taoist sage is unable to maintain that line here with any degree of certainty. Surely we are not permitted to look the other way while wrongdoers terrorise the community -whatever the consequences? Pucklechurch has quite a reputation for this sort of thing because it was here, in AD 946, that King Edmund was stabbed to death when he tried to prevent the 'atrocious robber' Liofa who was attacking his steward.

When I first saw the figure that emerged in the map of this route, it reminded me of Clarence the cross-eyed lion from Daktari, the TV series about vets in Africa from the 1970s, but that was just me showing my age! It actually looks much more like a leonine form of Janus the Roman god of thresholds who gave his name to January.

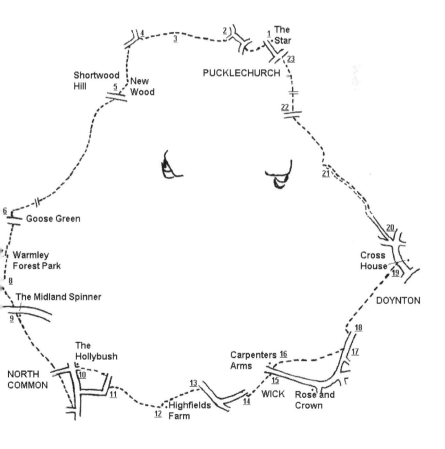

In the light of the saying from the Tao Te Ching, it is clear that the double-headed lion symbolises the two different forms of bravery, which might be summarised as the contrasting paths of self-sacrifice and self-denial. Neither option will appeal to those who choose to visit all the pubs on this route and drink to the memory of Bob Todd in each one.

If you do intend to drink, you should check out the timetable of the 689 bus service between Bristol and Yate, which calls at Pucklechurch. This is especially important if you get lured into trying all the ciders on offer at the Star at the end of your walk, because, if you do, you will understand what it is like to see the world through the eyes of Clarence the cross-eyed lion from Daktari!

> *Known Hazards: Brambles on Shortwood Hill*
> *Nettles at Goose Green*

FROM THE STAR TO THE MIDLAND SPINNER

From the Star **1**, head across the playing field opposite toward the church.

Make your way through the churchyard to the road.

Turn right and take the first road on the left.

After a couple of hundred metres, when road bends to the right, take a road on the left, which bends to the right to become a muddy track called King's Lane. **2**

Follow the track until it bends sharply to the left; go straight ahead (over a stile) into a field. **3**

In the field, bear left to a stile near the far left corner of the field. (Take care; it is further to the left than the distinct path that leads past a telegraph pole to a stile beside a gate.)

Turn right to a stile onto the road. **4**

Turn left and look for a stile into a field on the left.

In the field, go straight on along a tractor track, past a hedge corner to a gap in the hedge and a tall kissing-gate in a deer fence beyond.

Through the fence bear right down through the trees to another tall kissing gate and a wicket gate onto a major road. (This can be a struggle at the end of the summer when the path can get very overgrown.) **5**

Cross the road and turn right along the verge to find a stile into the field on the left.

In the field, bear right to a gate in the bottom right hand corner.

Through the gate, go straight-ahead, keeping a hedge on your right to a stile.

Over the stile, go straight ahead across a large field to find a kissing gate just below the middle of the opposite hedge. (It is just to the left of Warmley church spire in the distance.

In the next field, bear right to the lowest gap beside the golf course in the diagonally opposite corner.

Through the gap, make for a gate in the opposite side of a triangular field.

Through the gate, bear slightly left of a wooden electricity pole across the field to a kissing gate thirty metres from the field corner.

This kissing gate is on the line of a roman road.

In the next field, go straight-ahead, keeping the hedge on your right. (Look out for horse fences.)

Go through two kissing gates on either side of a track. In the next field, follow the left hand hedge to a mini gate in the corner.

Follow the nettly track up to a stile into a tarmac drive.

Go straight up the drive to the road at Goose Green. **6**

Cross Goose Green Road and turn left and immediately right down a drive to a kissing gate.

In the field, carry straight on along the hedge on your right to kissing gate.

Through the gate turn left and look for another kissing gate on the left. **7**

Through this gate, turn right and follow the right hand hedge along the edge of Warmley Forest Park.

Keep right until you reach a T-junction and turn right to a stile and gap beside a gate. **8**

Follow the path to the right of some trees to a Dramway signpost beside a road.

Turn sharply left into the dramway cutting, which directs you under a railway bridge onto the Dramway Path.

Follow the Dramway until it emerges onto the London Road opposite the **Midland Spinner**. **9**

This pub has improved beyond recognition, partly because of the introduction of the smoking ban. This has produced an attractive beer garden at the back, a much improved atmosphere inside and Bath Ales Gem on tap from the brewery round the corner.

FROM THE MIDLAND SPINNER TO THE HOLLYBUSH

Cross the road and turn left and then right down the Dramway Path between the builders' yard and the pub, unless you want a drink first.

Keep on the Dramway under a railway bridge and along an embankment and through a housing estate until you emerge on Poplar Road.

Turn left toward the **Hollybush** Public House, which will also have been improved by the smoking ban in my opinion. **10**

Cross the main road and go down the lane opposite unless you wish to visit the pub.

FROM THE HOLLYBUSH TO THE CARPENTERS' ARMS

Down the lane, turn left over a stile and right over another past some stables.

Keep right as you go straight ahead over double stiles toward a gate onto a road beside some rising ground.

Turn right and look for a kissing-gate on the left. **11** Go straight ahead through a pair of shin cracking mini-gates up the steep slope to another mini gate at the top.

Carry straight on along the plateau to one stile and straight on to the corner of the next field. **12**

Turn left over the stile and follow the diverted footpath to a kissing gate on the right.

Go through another kissing gate on the other side of the drive. Carry on past a pond to another kissing gate leading through a new willow avenue to yet another kissing gate.

Go down some steps through an attractive new plantation to a bridge and gate into old grassland above the River Boyd.

The age of the pasture is betrayed by the presence on anthills, which interrupt the path as it follows the contour to a gate into the next field.

Keep right to a kissing gate and an old stone stile onto the road. **13**

On the road, turn right over the river (Note the weir on your left.) and then left past Court Farm towards Wick Court.

Just before Wick Court, look for a stile up a short track into a field on the right. **14**

Turn left and follow the path behind Wick Court, which emerges between the houses ahead onto the main street in Wick. **15**

Turn left over Boyd Bridge if you want to visit the Carpenters' Arms. Otherwise turn right and then left towards the Golden Valley Nature Reserve.

Those of you who are observant and keen to get in an extra drink, will already have noticed a potential detour via the Rose and Crown.

FROM THE CARPENTERS' ARMS TO THE CROSS HOUSE

On the track up to the Nature reserve, take the first turning up a track on the right and look for a kissing gate on the left. **16**

Through the gate, bear right up the bank to a stile.

Go towards the house ahead to a kissing gate onto the lane.

Turn right down the lane and look for a stile on the left, just before the lane crosses the Lime Brook.

Follow the path through a narrow field and look for a stile in the fence ahead.

Over this stile, go straight ahead to a stile into the quarry compound. The path through the compound is well signed and enclosed for your safety; but you will need to keep your eyes open for lorries in a couple of places. There is only one place where the path is not immediately obvious, but you will be fine if you remember that the route is basically straight on to the exit. **17**

There is a permissive path on the left, immediately before the exit, which leads up some steps to a viewpoint over the quarry workings and a gate back onto the road.

Whether you go via the viewpoint or go left up the road past the gate, you are looking for a pedestrian gate on the left, which leads to a path through a field alongside the quarry. **18** Follow the quarry boundary fence on the left until a sign, shortly before a field gate ahead, indicates a path to the right. Turn right across the field, bearing slightly left, to a stile in the middle of the hedge opposite.

Over this stile, go straight ahead along the Monarch's Way over a stile in a stone wall, along a hedge, through a gap and another field to a stile into a green track.

Go straight ahead over a stile and across a field, used by local dog walkers, to a kissing gate and a path between the houses onto a road (High Street). **19** The Cross House pub is about fifty metres to the right. (If you do not wish to go to the pub, you can turn left on the green track onto a path that comes out down the High Street.)

FROM THE CROSS HOUSE TO THE STAR

Go down the High Street across the River Boyd to a road junction.

Turn left and then right past Wilkes' Farm **20** and follow the concrete road through the fields.

Keep going when the road deteriorates into a muddy track that leads to a ford.

You can avoid getting your feet wet (or even being swept away when the stream is swollen) by using the footbridge.

Turn right over a stile **21** and then left along a permissive footpath, which shadows the sometimes flooded track to a stile in the corner of the field.

Turn right and follow the hedge to a stile on the left.

Bear right to a kissing gate, and keep going, on the same line, through another kissing gate and across a large field to a gate in the far left hand corner.

Go through the gap beside the gate and another gap onto a road. **22**

Turn left and look for a kissing gate up some steps on the right.

Go straight across the field to a kissing gate onto another lane beside a cottage.

Go down the narrow footpath beside the cottage to a stile into a paddock and follow the right hand hedge onto a drive beside a house.

As the drive turns left, go straight ahead over a stile and across the next field to a stile onto a farm track.

Continue to the road **23** and turn left and then right up Castle Road.

The Star is up the road on the right.

9: GOLDEN VALLEY

OR 'TINTIN' - 7m (approx.)
From the Carpenters' Arms in Wick - ST702728

Pub Sign

Livery Company

The pub sign of the Carpenters' Arms in Wick closely resembles the seventeenth century coat of arms of the Carpenters' Livery Company in London, which is, in ordinary language: three black compasses and a black toothed chevron on a white background. The three compasses reveal a strong connection with the Masons and the three Masonic Virtues of Brotherly Love, Relief and Truth, illustrated in the drawing below.

The Masonic Virtues

These virtues can usefully be compared with those described in the twenty eighth chapter of the Tao Te Ching:

> *Know the strength of man*
> *But keep a woman's care.*
>> *Be the stream of the universe*
>> *Ever true and unswerving*
> *Become as a little child once more.*
> *Know the white.*
> *But keep to the black!*
>> *Be an example to the world.*

Being an example to the world
Ever true and unwavering
Return to the infinite.

Know honour.
Yet keep humility.
Be the Valley of the Universe
Being the Valley of the Universe
Return to the state of the uncarved block.

The coat of arms gives a new meaning to the lines: Know the white; but keep to the black. In the inn sign, the black refers to the compass and the white to the saw and chisel, which are the most obvious tools of a carpenter's trade. In the coat of arms of the livery company, the compasses are also black. I am reminded of the dictum, measure three times before you cut. The last verse also reminds us of masons and carpenters with its reference to the uncarved block.

The first verse seemed a little harder to place until the profile of Hergé's cartoon character, Tintin, appeared in the route map.

The Belgian boy detective, Tintin showed fictional courage reminiscent of the real life courage of the innkeeper in the last chapter. This is appropriate, since this route covers some of the same ground.

'Tintin in Tibet' was the author Hergé's favourite. In that story, Tintin was summoned by a dream to search for his Chinese friend Chang - lost after a plane crash in the Himalayas. There, Tintin and his friends landed up in a religious Shangri-La, a Tibetan monastery in a valley free from snow, a veritable Golden Valley. The abbot of the monastery gave Tintin a yellow silk scarf in token of his courage and the strength of his brotherly love towards Chang. The real life Dalai Lama gave the Hergé foundation 'The Light of Truth Award', for their defence of the integrity of the book in the face of Chinese revision.

The Golden Valley nature reserve and the River Boyd supply the missing references to 'the Valley of the Universe' and the Stream of the Universe'.

Food and drink are available en route at the much improved Midland Spinner in Warmley or at the Snax bar on the station of the Railway Path (open seven days a week from about 10 till 5 except for the winter when it only opens at the weekend) or at Silvo's Food Bar, which is open during the working week at the Build Center next to the pub, and also on your return to the Carpenters' Arms.

The 634 and 635 bus services both serve Wick. These also stop at Warmley, which is served in addition by the 43, 43a and 319.

Known hazards: Steep hazardous climb at Golden Valley Reserve
Steep descent with steps at Highfield Farm
Severe nettles at (3) (Ketcheshill Farm)

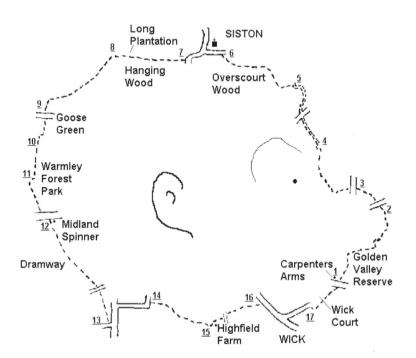

FROM THE CARPENTERS' ARMS TO THE MIDLAND SPINNER

From the Carpenters' Arms **1**, turn left and cross Boyd Bridge. Over the bridge, turn left and follow Golden Valley Road to a squeeze beside a gate into the Golden Valley nature reserve.

Follow the track until you cross a bridge over the River Boyd on the left.

Turn right and follow the Ochre Trail along the tarmac path along the other side of the river. Or follow the other trails along the valley bottom, which explore the site of the old ochre works, which used to exploit the pigment produced from local iron oxides.

At the end of the path, admire the view of the river foaming over a weir and climb the steps beside the water fall to gain a better view.

Carry on up the steps past the viewpoint to the top and continue up a rough, narrow stony, dangerous path, which winds up to the right alongside the edge of a cliff on the right. Continue to right, whilst avoiding paths that appear to go over the edge of the cliff, until you reach a kissing gate into a field ahead.

Turn right and descend to a view point across the river and the quarry, known as Raven's Rock.

If you wish to avoid this dangerous climb up to the Raven's Rock, follow the Raven's Rock trail over the bridge.

Take the right fork up a track that winds up through the wood to a kissing gate into a field.

In the field, bear right to a gap into another field.

Follow the right hand hedge to a kissing gate, which allows access to the Raven's Rock view point.

After you have admired the view, turn left and follow the path alongside the quarry edge. Keep to the fence on the path that drops steeply down a slippery slope and up the other side to emerge through a stone arch. (The left hand path avoids the slippery path and this arch.)

Turn right on the distinct track to another arch, through which you follow the quarry edge to a track past some houses onto a road. **2**

Over the road, climb the stile into a field.

Bear left to find a kissing gate past the end of the hedge on the left.

Through the kissing gate, bear right to find two kissing gates in the corner of the field onto the road opposite Ketcheshill Farm. **3**

Go over the stone stile beside the tall wooden gate to the left of the farm and over a wooden stile into a narrow path filled with nettles.

 Go through some field gates into a field and go straight ahead to the corner.

Do not use the stile on the left, but turn right and keep going with the hedge on your left to a hedge corner. (You will probably have to negotiate some electric horse tapes on the way.)

At the hedge corner, keep going straight ahead across the field to a difficult stile in the hedge corner opposite.

Over the stile, follow the left hand hedge to a new kissing gate hidden in the corner.

Go through a vegetable garden and over a stile then turn right onto the drive to Clovermead Farm. **4**

Turn left and follow the drive to a road. Cross the road into the track opposite.

Look for a kissing gate into the field on the right and bear right to look for a new wicket gate in the diagonally opposite corner, where I saw a little owl.

In the next field, go straight ahead along the left hand hedge. *This field was overgrown with grass in the wet summer of 2007 and concealed a pair of young roe deer, which only got up when I nearly trod on them.*

Round a corner of the hedge, look for a stile and bridge on the left. Over the stile, follow the left hand hedge to a field gate into the next field. Bear right to a kissing gate near a building. The path was beautifully mown in 2007.

Through this kissing gate, bear right, to another kissing gate.
This field and the next were stocked with alpacas and vicunas that year. These are smaller versions of the llamas, which featured in 'Tintin and the Prisoners of the Sun'. I believe the alpacas are the white woolly ones and the vicunas are chestnut coloured, but I am no expert.

Follow the path past the house ahead into the drive to emerge in a road beside a sign for Avon Alpacas.**6**

Turn left to a road junction below the parish church. At the major road, turn left (or straight on -it depends on your point of view!)

As the road bends to the left go straight on to a stile into some access land. **7**

Go straight on up the hill to an old field-boundary.

On the plateau, (or clearing) go straight ahead - keep right of the first set of new trees, and head for the gap between two more new plantations - to a kissing gate on the right in the opposite corner of the field.

Look back as you pass the first plantation to see the Elizabethan House, Siston Court, above the parish church. It is a shame it does not look more like Marlinspike Hall, the house of Tintin's heavy-drinking friend, Captain Haddock.

Through the gate, turn left to a gap in the hedge.

Through the gap, keep going downhill with a hedge on your left to the last gap on the left at the bottom of the hill.

Turn left through the gap to join The Community Forest Path. **8**
Make for a field gate in the opposite side of the triangular field. (It is becoming a little overgrown and hard to see.)

Through the gate, bear slightly left across the field to a kissing gate fifty metres from the field corner.

As you climb this stile, you are crossing the line of the Roman Road from Gloucester to a junction with the road from Bath to Sea Mills near Bitton Station.

In the next field, go straight-ahead, keeping the hedge on your right. (Look out for horse fences. Last time, there were two improvised gates.)

Go through two kissing gates on either side of a track.

In the next field, follow the left hand hedge to a shin trap gate in the corner.

Through the gate, follow a nettly track to a step-over onto a tarmac drive.

Go straight up the drive to the road (Goose Green). **9**

In Goose Green turn left and then right up a drive (past a house called Brooklyn) to a kissing gate into field.

In the field, follow the right hand hedge to find a kissing gate on the right.

Through the gate, turn left and look for a kissing gate on the left. **10**

Through the gate, turn right and follow the hedge downhill until you come to a gap in a fence.

Through the gap, follow a gravely track for a bout 50m to a path off to the right, which leads to a gate.

Through the gate, go straight ahead past a group of trees, over a track and downhill past some houses to a Dramway signpost. **11**

Turn left onto the Dramway path, which goes under a railway bridge and follow it down to the main road, keeping the hedge on your right.

Cross the Main Road and turn left past a builders' yard to find an unprepossessing path between some industrial buildings just before the Midland Spinner. **12**.

Turn down this path unless you are visiting the pub.

FROM THE MIDLAND SPINNER TO THE CARPENTERS' ARMS

The path opens out into a railway cutting, which is shaded by trees. On the downside it can be muddy, especially under a railway bridge.

This is, in my opinion, the most evocative section of the Dramway footpath, which runs from Coalpit Heath, in the Coalpit Heath/Parkfield Coalfield to Londonderry Wharf on the River Avon.

Keep on the line of the Dramway Path through some new housing, which shows the line of the old railway across the grass, and down a gravel path between factory units to emerge at a T-junction in Southway Drive. **13**

On Southway Drive turn left to a main road.

On the main road, turn left and then right down the first turning on the right.

Follow the road round a bend to the left past a farmhouse. Then look for a kissing gate on the right. **14**

Through the gate, go straight ahead, with the hedge on your left, through two shin trap gates and up a steep slope to another shin trap at the top of the escarpment.

Over the shin trap, continue over the brow of hill, keeping a hedge on your left to a wooden stile.

There is a beautiful view ahead, and you should be able to make out the distinctive row of beeches on the ridge of Freezing Hill.

Carry on until you reach a stile in a wall on the left, which marks the beginning of a diversion around Highfield Farm. **15**

The diversion goes through a pair of kissing gates across the farm drive, past a pond to another kissing gate, through some newly planted willows and across some grass to a kissing gate at the top of a steep descent down some steps and over a boardwalk to another gate.

Through the gate, follow tracks left by Jacob's sheep below the left hand hedge to find a gate behind some hawthorn bushes in the corner.

Through the gate, bear slightly right of straight-ahead to a gate and a stone stile onto the road. **16**

On the road turn right and then left past Court Farm towards Wick Court, *an early seventeenth century manor house, built by Sir Edward Wintour - which is also not much like Marlinspike Hall!*

Just past Briar Cottage and the wall of the garden of Wick Court, look for a stile into a green lane on the right. **17**

At the end of the short lane, turn left over a stone stile into a field and follow the boundary at the back of Wick Court to a stile.

Over this stile, go straight across the field to a path between the houses onto the road at Boyd Bridge.

You should now be able to see the Carpenters' Arms on the left.

Another route, which explores the Golden Valley and visits the Carpenters' Arms and the Midland Spinner, can be found at www.closertothecountryside.co.uk. It is called 'Golden Valley Pits' and starts beside the County Bridge at Keynsham at the Lockkeeper, a pub, which also features in the two following routes.

10: HANGING HILL
OR 'THE HANGMAN' -nearly 12 miles
From the Swan at Swineford -ST690691

The Swan is one of the few pubs in the Bath Ales stable, which is out in the countryside. The typical Bath Ales pub is a twenty-first century version of a traditional town boozer, with a selection of classy real ales and pub grub well above the average. The Swan continues this tradition in a rural setting, and has the additional advantage that it is ideally placed for walks along the river and up into the hills behind. Parking used to be hazardous at 'The Swan', but the judicious purchase of a piece of land from a neighbouring farmer means that there is now room for a pub car park as well as an extensive beer garden for people with children or a smoking habit.

It is an odd fact that the surname of one of the directors of Bath Ales (Richard Dempster) means "The officer of a Scottish court who pronounced doom or sentence definitively as directed by the clerk or judge," according to the Shorter Oxford Dictionary. But it is probably just a coincidence that "Dempstered" means hanged according to the Cassell Dictionary of Slang and that the image of a hooded hangman appears on the map of this route.

This chain of coincidences is continued by the fact that the section between the Swan and the Carpenters' Arms crosses over Hanging Hill, although the hill itself is a glorious viewpoint in a wooded landscape with access land on either side. It is written in the Tao Te Ching:

> *If men are not afraid to die,*
> *It is of no avail to threaten them with death…*
>
> *There is always an official executioner.*
> *If you try to take his place,*
> *It is like trying to be a master carpenter and cutting wood.*
> *If you try to cut wood like a master carpenter,*
> *You will only hurt your hand.*

So the Carpenters' Arms provides another unexpected connection with the theme.

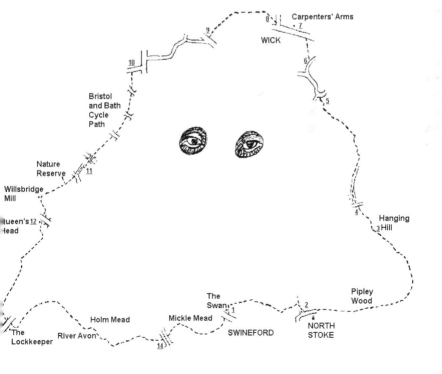

Refreshments are available at the Queen's Head at Willsbridge and the Lockkeeeper beside the County Bridge at Keynsham as well as at the Carpenters and the Swan.

If you wish to use public transport, it is worth checking out the timetable of the 319 and the 332 between Bristol and Bath, which both pass the Swan.

FROM THE SWAN TO THE CARPENTERS' ARMS

From the pub car park, **1** follow the track up towards a public picnic area.

Just before you reach it, turn right between a stone wall and a mill leat, in which you can hear the sound of gurgling water as it passes beneath you.

Go over one stile and on to a double stile into a rising field.

Follow the path up the spur of the hill to a stile into an enclosed track.

Follow the rocky track up the hill and around a right angled bend to the left until you reach a distinct junction. Ignore the distinctively named Pipley Bottom to your left and turn right between some houses.

When you reach a tarmac road **(2)**, turn left and follow the road up to a church.

Bear left on a stony track around the church that winds up past some farm buildings to a gate across it. **(Please keep the gate shut.)**

Through the gate, carry on up the track through a long, rising, grassy field to another gate across.

You are now on a section of the Cotswold Way. The woodland on the left called Pipley Wood is open to the public.

Carry on up the track to a junction in the middle of a golf course and turn left.

Follow the yellowish track alongside a wood on the right and round the end of the fairway to a small gate.

Through the gate, follow the hedge on your left through some pine trees to a kissing gate. Keep going through the remains of a shallow quarry to another kissing gate beside a trig point and a metal flag marking the edge of the escarpment of Hanging Hill. **3**

Hanging Hill formed the western flank of the Parliamentary position at the Battle of Lansdown during the Civil War in 1643. The Royalists won the engagement, but they suffered such severe losses that they were not able to take advantage of their victory. Their leader, Sir Bevil Grenville was killed and his monument can be seen near Lansdown Road further along the escarpment.

Leave the Cotswold Way at the kissing gate and descend the escarpment, following the left hand hedge as best you can through the rough grass and scrub until you find a hunting gate into a distinct enclosed and rocky track. **(Take care! The usual roots and loose stones are complimented by dangerous, natural sloping steps toward the bottom.)**

When you emerge at a road junction (**4**) go straight ahead on the road signposted to Beach. Carry straight ahead when the road bends sharply to the left down a 'no through road'

Keep going straight ahead as the lane deteriorates into a stony track past some impressive looking gateposts.

Carry on through some woods and across a ford until you emerge, after about a kilometre, past Coldharbour Farm on a tarmac road **5**.

Turn left, go straight on past one junction and bear right at the second.

After three hundred metres, look for a stone stile on the left into a field **6**. (This is the second stile. Do not be mislead by the tempting gate, which leads to an electricity sub station, or the signed path, which leads alongside a stream. The one you need is on the rise on the other side of the stream, and you may have to bash down some nettles to reach it.)

Go straight ahead across the paddock to a wooden stile and then bear quite sharply right to another. Keep going downhill to find a path between the houses near the corner of the field, which leads through to a main road.

Cross over and turn left to the Carpenters' Arms in Wick. **7**

FROM THE CARPENTERS' ARMS TO THE LOCKKEEPER

From the pub, go past the car park and follow the footpath alongside some houses towards some traffic lights and cross over to a stone stile into an enclosed footpath.

Turn left across a bridge into a playing field.

Bear right across the field to a kissing gate in a hedge corner. **8**

Turn right and follow the path up hill through two kissing gates. Bear left under some power lines and follow the hedge on your right past one kissing gate and through a gap in a hedge. Near the summit of the hill, look for a stile in the hedge. On the other side turn left to a gateway.

Through the gate, the right of way is shown on the map cutting the corner of the field to another gate under some more power lines, but when I was there last, the field was ploughed and there was an obvious grass headland around the edge of the field.

Through the next gate, follow the left hand hedge down to a major road. *(Caution A420!)* **9**

Cross the road and turn down the track behind the cottages opposite.

Follow the track downhill until it joins a minor road.

Turn left and follow the lane for about six hundred metres until you come to a major road.

Cross the road and turn left to look for the first turning on the right (Southway Drive).

Go straight ahead for about two hundred metres and then turn left onto the cycle track. **10**

Follow the path until the Avon Valley Railway starts at Oldland Common.

Count three bridges overhead, including the one just before the railway starts.

Then, just after the railway path goes <u>over</u> a bridge, turn up some steps right into a residential street. **11**

Follow the street to T-junction and then look for a kissing gate ahead and to the right into the Willsbridge Valley Nature Reserve.

Follow the path past the bottom of the California Incline through a gate to Willsbridge Mill.

At the Mill, continue alongside the stream through the 'ecological' garden to emerge opposite the Queen's Head. **12**

Cross the road and then turn right into the pub car park.

Over the stile at the far end of the car park, follow the line of Siston Brook on your left.

Negotiate the ruts and bumps created by generations of cattle until you reach a stile. Keep following the Brook along a section where it is worth keeping your eyes open for kingfishers to a set of gates leading to the banks of the River Avon.

Turn left along the riverbank past Londonderry Wharf, which was the terminus of the Dramway.

Follow the river bank through a long meadow, called Sydenham Mead, usually stocked with sheep in the summer.

Sydenham Mead was the site of a skirmish between troops loyal to James II and Monmouth's Rebels. It was not much of a battle, but it prompted the Duke of Monmouth's fatal decision to retreat back into Somerset, rather than cross the river and march on Bristol, whose defences had been dismantled on Cromwell's orders after the Civil War. This led to Monmouth's defeat at the Battle of Sedgemoor and the Bloody Assizes conducted by Judge Jefferies to root out those sympathetic to the rebels. Those who were not hanged were transported as slaves to the West Indies, which was the start of Bristol's involvement with the slave trade.

It is written in the Tao Te Ching:

> *There is a saying among soldiers:*
> *I dare not make the first move, but would rather play the guest.*
> *I dare not advance an inch, but would rather withdraw a foot.*
> *This is called marching without appearing to move,*
> *Rolling up your sleeves without showing your arm,*
> *Capturing the enemy without attacking,*
> *Being armed without weapons.*
> *There is no greater catastrophe than underesti mating the enemy.*
> *By underestimating the enemy, I almost lose what I value.*
> *Therefore, when battle is joined,*
> *The underdog will win.*

- which goes to show that if you want military advice, you would do better to consult 'The Art of War' by Sun Tzu, who was a soldier rather than a hermit!

Just before you get to the Lockkeeper, (13) you will notice a new plantation. This is Sydenham Mead plantation, which was planted in association with the Forest of Avon by children from Wellsway School and Temple County Primary.

FROM THE LOCKKEEPER TO THE SWAN

Follow the path over the footbridge across the entrance to the marina and follow the river until the path emerges onto a track.

Turn right and follow the track over a cattle grid and then just follow the river bank for just over two miles back to the Swan at Swineford.

You will pass the original terminus of the Dramway, beside a pipeline, which crosses the river between some houseboats. The only other major feature is the Bristol and Bath Railway bridge at Riverside Station. <u>14</u> *This is the terminus of the Avon Valley Railway. There is also a mooring for a river bus, which sails along the river from Keynsham during the summer.*

The pub is a kilometre past the bridge.

11: RIVERSIDE STATION
OR 'THE SMOKING PIG' -6.5 miles
From the Lockkeeper at County Bridge, Keynsham - ST659690

This route, which combines two riverside walks with a visit to one of the community forests promoted by the Forest of Avon Team, begins at the Lockkeeper beside the County Bridge on the A4175 from Willsbridge to Keynsham. This is a Young's pub, so the beer is good and the food is popular too, which makes it crowded at times. The only other thing that was ever wrong with the pub was the cigarette smoke in the bar, a fault that has now been cured!

The image of a pig, which seems to be smoking a section of the A4, has appeared in the map of this route. I should imagine he does not fancy the idea of being cured at all. Being a pig, he would rather save his bacon!

It is written in the Tao:

> *Knowing ignorance is strength.*
> *Ignoring knowledge is sickness.*

These wise words from the Tao Te Ching are very nearly all you need to know. The first line refers to the limits of knowledge. The main purpose of taking a university degree is to learn this lesson, although I am not at all sure that it is taught effectively in all courses. The second line refers to the fact that we ignore at our peril inconvenient truths, such as the effects of tobacco and cannabis on the body and mind, or the effects on the planet of a planning system based on the private car. The observant among you will have noticed that I make no mention of alcohol!

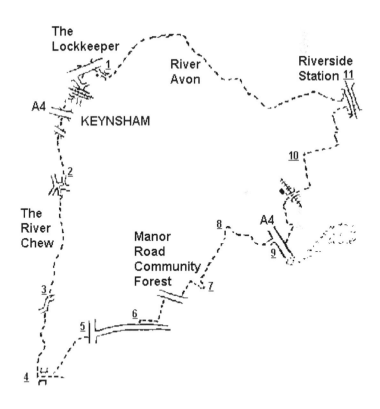

A pig smoking a spliff!? It is many years since I have seen such a thing!

FROM THE LOCKKEEPER TO CHEWTON KEYNSHAM ON THE FOREST PATH

From the Lockkeeper **1**, get onto the main road into Keynsham (A 4175), turn left and cross the County Bridge over the River Avon.

Take first turning on the left and then first right under a railway arch.

On the far side, go through a gate on the right into a park and bear right down the hill to a footbridge over the River Chew.

Turn left and follow the river upstream, as closely as you can (for about half a mile -under a bridge and through parks and a spinney) until you emerge in a cul-de-sac. **2**

At the junction at the other end of the cul-de-sac, turn right and then left.

Turn left again where path goes through an old people's home to the riverside.

Follow the river as closely as you can until it emerges on a road on a blind corner. **3**

Go straight ahead down the road, turn left into a field, go over a small bridge and follow the riverbank to a double-gate into another field.

In this field go straight ahead to a kissing gate into a track. **4**

FROM CHEWTON KEYNSHAM TO THE RIVERSIDE STATION VIA THE MANOR ROAD COMMUNITY WOOD

In the track, turn left and then left again at the first junction. Follow the track uphill to a major road. **5**

Cross the road into Courtnay Road and follow it out into the countryside.

Just after the last house on the left, look for a kissing gate into **The Community Woodland. 6**

Turn right alongside the hedge and then left along a bridle path to emerge in Manor Road.

In the road, turn right and then left into another section of the wood.

Turn right and then left alongside a wall to the bottom of the plantation.

Turn right and go straight on across an open space to pick up a hedge on your left.

Look for a hunting gate in this hedge. (It is usually propped open.) **7**

Through the gate, turn left through a gap and then right along a permissive path, keeping a hedge on your right.

At end of the field, turn left and then right through a field gate. **8**

Through the gate, turn right to a stile. (The stile is unnecessary as there is an open gate next to it.)

Keep straight on to a concrete track.

Turn right and then left over a stile. (This stile was also supernumerary last time I saw it!)

Follow a diagonal path to a stile into a cul-de-sac leading to the main Bristol to Bath road. **9**

Turn right to a very necessary pedestrian refuge.

 Cross the road and turn right again to find a kissing gate on the left. (Watch out! There was an electric fence on the other side last time I was there.)

 Through the kissing gate, bear slightly left to a kissing gate beside a field gate. (Caution is again required to avoid the barbed wire on the other side.)

Through the gate, turn left and follow the track around the corner of the field to a gate onto another track on the left. (Beware cow dung!)

In this track, turn immediately right up an enclosed permissive path to a bridge over the railway.

Over the railway, turn right to a field corner and then left along a rough track towards Avon Farm.

Before the farm, turn right through a gate. **10**

Follow the field boundary round to the right, with the hedge on your left to a stile in the corner of the field.

Go straight on with a hedge on your right to a double stile through the hedge.

Over the stiles, turn left along the other side of hedge down to the bottom of the field.

I have found worked flints in this field, just before the slope down to the river becomes marked. I suspect that they mark the site of a Stone Age settlement on the flat ground above the boggy ground, liable to flood.

Follow the path right handed towards the river and the follow the river toward the railway bridge.

In the field corner, make your way up to the right onto the Bristol & Bath Railway Path at Avon Riverside Station. **11**

This is the terminus of the Avon Valley Railway, which is based at Willsbridge on the A431between Hanham and Bitton. See www.avonvalleyrailway.org for an up to date timetable. This also gives details of boat trips from the quay down by the riverside in the summer.

FROM THE RIVERSIDE STATION TO THE LOCKKEEPER ALONG THE RIVER AVON

On the Railway Path, turn left and cross the River Avon. Then turn left down a track to the riverboat mooring and turn right.

Follow the river as closely as you can over a series of stiles until you reach a field track.

Follow the track to a cattle grid.

Cross the stile beside it and look out for a path on the left, which follows the riverbank, over a footbridge at the entrance to a marina and on to the Lockkeeper.

12: STANTONBURY HILL FORT
OR 'THE WOOD WIGHT' -7.5 miles +
From the Compton Inn at Compton Dando - ST646646

The fact that Compton Dando is an excellent centre for walking, running and riding is a poorly kept secret. The Compton Inn, now refurbished and developing a reputation for its food, has been for some years the start and finish of a very popular multi-terrain running race, the Compton Dandy Run, put on by the Town and Country Harriers running club as part of their Summer Pub Series. (This route follows the first mile of the race course.) In addition, the section between Compton and Chewton is often crammed with dog-walkers and I have seen bat watchers out walking here too.

The route returns to the Chew near Chewton Keynsham through an area criss-crossed by new permissive bridle paths negotiated by Defra with local farmers between Saltford and Keynsham as part of the Countryside Stewardship Scheme. There are other bridle paths in the Manor Road Community Woodland, which must link with these.

The theme of this route is supplied by Stantonbury, one of the hill forts on the Wansdyke, the mysterious Dark Age linear feature along the high country to the south of the Avon Valley.

Knowing the ancient beginning is the essence of Tao.

The Wansdyke has been traced for about eighty miles from Walbury Hill near Hungerford to the site of a fort at the western end of the Wansdyke near Portishead. Much of the route is controversial. And its date and purpose have not been established beyond reasonable doubt. However, Dr Ken Dark expressed the expert opinion that it was constructed by a Romano British statelet in the fifth or sixth century (in an interview, which can be found at www.wansdyke21.org.uk, probably the most convenient place to find out more about the Wansdyke.)

The route map shows a ghostly figure sneaking menacingly across the countryside. I believe it may be a wood-wight

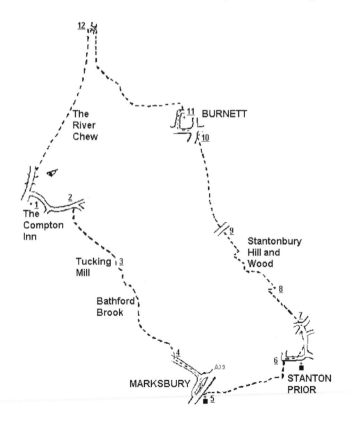

What is a wood wight?
> *Look it cannot be seen -it is beyond form.*
> *Listen, it cannot be heard -it is beyond sound.*
> *Grasp, it cannot be held -it is intangible.*
> *These three are indefinable;*
> *Therefore they are joined in one.*

> *From above it is not bright;*
> *From below it is not dark;*
> *An unbroken thread beyond description.*
> *It returns to nothingness.*
> *The form of the formless,*
> *The image of the imageless,*
> *It is called indefinable and beyond imagination.*

'It' is the Tao of course, but the lines could apply equally well to a wood wight, a creature that might well inhabit an ancient wooded site like Stantonbury fort.
The village is not well served by the buses, but the 640 service between Keynsham and Chew Stoke does visit less frequently than six days a week. An hourly service (no 178) stops in Marksbury so bus users ought to start from there.

FROM THE COMPTON INN TO MARKSBURY

From the pub **1**, turn right and right again down the road signposted to Burnett and Stanton Prior.

When the road forks, turn right off the road down a track. **2** Follow the track, which ends up following a streambed. (There is an alternative path alongside the stream, but it is often nettled.)

Climb the stile straight ahead at the end of the water and follow the track around the bend to the left past a group of houses called Tucking Mill and look for a stile on the right into an enclosed path. **3**

This path is unstable underfoot and is liable to get overgrown. However, it is possible to bypass the path by climbing the stile beside the cattle grid and going through the field to rejoin the path on the other side of a second stile.

117

Follow the right hand fence through the field to a stile 50m up from the field corner.

In the next field, follow the right hand hedge alongside the Markham Brook to a hedge corner.

Go straight ahead across the field to a cart track, which follows a hedge on the left to a gate.

Through the gate, go straight ahead along the left hand hedge to a gate on the left.

Through the gate, carry on, on the same line, up an enclosed track towards a barn.

Just before the barn, turn left over a stile, and follow the track around the back of the buildings and up to a stile to the left next to a gate. **4**

Over this stile, turn right on an enclosed track down to another stile beside a gate onto the road beside Court Farm, Marksbury Vale.

Follow the lane up to T-junction past a chapel on the right.

Your aim is to go straight ahead up a lane past the village nursery, which involves turning right, left and right again.

Past the nursery, turn right on the pavement alongside the A39 towards Marksbury Church.

Cross the road to a stile on the left just before the churchyard into an area of community woodland. **5**

FROM MARKSBURY TO BURNETT

In the new planting, follow the clear grassy path diagonally to the left through the trees to a stile into a field.

Over the stile, head fractionally right of straight ahead to another stile and across the next field to yet another.

In the next field, the path follows a hedge on the left to a gate.

Over the gate, go straight ahead to a farm track and turn left along it to another gate, which gets very muddy in the winter. **6**

Turn right along the road, into Stanton Prior, past a sign telling you that a footpath has been diverted to a metalled path beside some houses on the left.

When the path emerges in the road, turn left and follow it past junctions on either side and a farmhouse B&B to a kissing gate into a field straight ahead. **7**

In the field, follow the distinct path across the field to a hedge corner.

Past the corner, turn right and left through a gap and follow the left hand hedge up to the corner of the field beside a wood.

Turn right alongside the wood to a kissing gate on your left. **8**

Bear left on a path up through the trees crossing a forestry track on the way up to emerge in a clearing at the top of the hill. *This clearing is in the middle of Stantonbury, an Iron Age hill fort, whose outlines are now obscured by surrounding woods, the imaginary haunt of wood wights.*

Go straight across to a track along the other side and turn left. *In the winter it ought to be possible to see across to Maes Knoll, but it was too misty when I tried it.*

Follow the wood-side until you reach a track down through the wood on the right. (Ignore the first post on your right, which looks as if it ought to carry a footpath sign. The correct path is in the corner of the clearing.)

The path follows a hollow lane down through the wood, which has been interpreted as the line of the Wansdyke, a Dark Age structure of unknown date and purpose.

After the path crosses a forestry track, the hollow lane becomes impassable and the waymarked route bears right through the trees to a stile. Following the route involved clambering over fallen trees when I checked it last.

Over the stile, go straight across the field to a gate onto the road. **9**

Cross over the road to a stile and follow the path parallel to a road on the left over three stiles.

Past the third stile, follow the hedge on the right to a hedge corner and then bear left across the field towards a kissing gate beside some houses. **10**

Turn right along the A39. As you will have discovered already, this is a busy road, and there is no pavement on the near side of the road. Also the path on the other side does not start for fifty metres, so you may prefer to stay in the field until you reach the gate in the corner of the field.

In any case, you need to turn left across the road into Burnett village.

FROM BURNETT TO COMPTON DANDO

Take the first lane on your right past St Michael's Church, which appears to be a funerary chapel.

After the road bends to the right past a stream on the right, turn left beside one cottage up a track bearing the sign 'War Cottage' to a stile. **11**

Over the stile turn left along a track alongside a wire to a gap beside a triangular wood.

Through the gap, bear right down the hill to a gap beside another wood.

Turn right alongside the wood to the corner.

From this point, the right of way heads slightly left of straight ahead across the field down to a kissing gate beside the river Chew. This path is rarely used and is often overgrown with crops. There is a track around the edge of the field, but this makes your journey to the kissing gate more than twice as long.

Through the kissing gate, follow the Chew downstream to another onto a rough track.

Turn left on the track and cross the River Chew.

Over the bridge, turn left through a kissing gate. **12**

You are now on the Community Forest Path and the Two Rivers Way.

Follow the riverbank to a plank bridge and stile.

Over the stile, follow the river to a kissing gate.

Through the kissing gate, bear right to a kissing gate on the horizon.

Turn left to a bridge and another kissing gate. (The bridge is not very obvious on the ground as the rivulet has been culverted under it.

Through the gate follow the track alongside a grassy bank (there are cowslips in spring) to a kissing gate into a wood.

At the end of the wood, go straight ahead to a kissing gate at the end of the field beside the river.

Through the gate, follow the riverbank to yet another kissing gate.

In the next field, the path shadows the line of the right hand hedge to a kissing gate onto the road.

Turn left and follow the road over the Chew to **the Compton Inn.**

For more information about wood wights and their cousins the woodwoses check out:

www.closertothecountryside.co.uk .

13: LORDS AND COMMONS
OR 'THE GIMP' -about 8 miles
From the Old Lockup in Pensford -ST620637

The route starts from the Old Lockup in Pensford, which is a tiny listed building at the junction between the High Street and the road to Publow and Woollard. It is chiefly famous as the place where legendary jazz clarinettist, Acker Bilk, started the gruelling Pensford 10K road race. It was designed to hold rowdy miners, possibly under the influence of the beer and cider available from the George and Dragon and the Rising Sun in Pensford. There is a third pub, the Traveller's Rest on the way into the village from Bristol, which is a little further off the route.

The route is called Lords and Commons, because it goes through the mature woodland at Lord's Wood and Common Wood. It also links these to the Community Forest Path and to the new plantation of Wooscombe Wood and follows stretches of the Markham Brook and the River Chew.

It is subtitled The Gimp because the sketch map resembles an unfortunate, being dragged off, bound and gagged, to the lockup as part of some SM fantasy.

It reminds us to

> *Accept disgrace willingly.*
> *Accept misfortune as the human condition.*

Personally, I believe that whether we are lords or commoners, we all come to the same end, so pride and humility are equally misplaced.

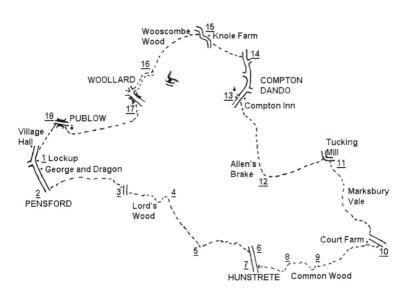

If you are travelling by bus, the 375, 376 and 379 buses all stop at Pensford Bridge.
Parking is scarce in the village, but I have been advised that it all right to park in the car park of the village hall. (If you approach on the A37 from Bristol, turn left when you cross the bridge and left again for village hall.) There is also parking opposite the Rising Sun and there are a couple of spaces next to the bus stop on the main road.

Food and drink can be obtained at the Compton Inn (recently refurbished, with special attention being paid to the kitchen) as well as at the George and Dragon and at the Rising Sun in Pensford.

FROM THE OLD LOCKUP TO LORDS' WOOD

From the lockup (**1**), go up the hill past the George and Dragon to look for a path just past a post box in a wall on the left. **2**

Go through a kissing gate into the field, and follow the remains of a hedge in a gully on the right to an oak tree at the top of a ridge.

Go straight ahead down the slope to a find a kissing gate hidden in a bend in the hedge below. This is quite hard to find. It is helpful to look out for the wooded slopes of Stantonbury Hill next to a barer hill in the distance and head a few degrees to the right of the bare hill towards a nearer wood. The kissing gate, which leads to a bridge and stile over a rivulet, is marked by a dying alder tree.

In the next field, follow the right hand hedge past a solitary oak tree to find a pair of stiles on the right.

Turn left down the other side of the hedge to a stile into a wood.

Follow the path down through the wood to a stream and a pair of stiles into a field.

Follow the right hand hedge up the slope to emerge over a stile into Birchwood Lane. **3**

Turn right and then left into Lord's Wood, admiring another view of Stantonbury Hill over a gate on the way.

Descend the ride to a junction at which you turn left and immediately right down a steep path, which becomes overgrown and squelchy towards the bottom as it approaches a pond.

This pond in the middle of Lord's Wood is remembered fondly by a set of runners in a TACH race, who mistakenly thought they were supposed to wade across it. I wouldn't fancy it! TACH (or Town and Country Harriers) put on a popular Summer Pub Series of cross country races, one of which begins at the Compton Inn.

Do not go straight on into the pond, like the runners in the first Compton Dandy Race, but follow the left bank of the pond round to the other side.

Turn left down a path to a major track junction and go straight up the track opposite to a kissing gate at the top of the wood. **4**

LORD'S WOOD TO COMMON WOOD

Through the gate turn right down the side of the wood to a stile over a wooden bridge at the bottom of some steps, which are usually hidden behind a wall of bracken and nettles at the end of the summer.

Go up some more steps to another stile into the next field and turn left up the fence side to a pair of stiles on the left.

Over this stile, go straight ahead along the hedge on your right to the corner of the field by a gate. **5**

This is labelled Pete's Gate 1991 for some reason.

Turn left and follow the hedge down to another gate, which is now redundant as a fence has been grubbed up.

Follow the right hand hedge down the hill and look for a kissing gate on the right.

Through the gate, follow the hedge round the left hand edge of the field to a stile next to a gate onto the road. **6**

Technically, the right of way cuts the corners of this and the last field. Some people like to stick rigidly to their rights, but this is only sensible if the cropping allows it. Similarly, the stile is overgrown, but the gate is missing, so anyone who cut the corner should logically force their way over the stile!

Turn right into the village. Pass the Victorian letterbox and footpath sign on your right. Then, as a red telephone box comes into view, look for a track next to Sarah's Cottage on the left, which leads to a wicket gate into a field. **7**

Descend past some electricity poles to a stile into Common Wood.

Follow the path down from the stile to a stony track through the wood.

Follow the track, past Bristol Outdoor Pursuits Centre's 'Hamburger Hill' paint-balling facility. **8**

Keep to the track, ignoring tracks off into the paint-balling area as it bends first to the right and then to the left

Ignore, too, a track through a gate on the right and look for a signed footpath on the right, which leads up through the trees to a field.

FROM COMMON WOOD TO COMPTON DANDO

In the field, turn left along the side of the wood to a corner. **9**

Turn right to a solitary ash tree and then turn left to follow the edge of a rough patch over the brow of the hill and straight across the field to a path through some bushes to a stile at the top of an escarpment.

Descend alongside the left hand hedge to a sign which indicates a diversion of the footpath to the right around the garden and buildings of Court Farm below.

Go over a stile next to a gate, which leads to a green track beside a pond, to emerge in a no-through road. **10**

Turn left, and look for a stile on the right just before you reach the farm buildings.

Follow the track around the buildings to another stile next to a gate, and descend the track around the buildings that emerges by the back entrance to a barn.

Follow the track away from the barn to look for a gate into a field on the left.

Through the gate, follow the right hand hedge for the full length of the field to another gate.

Follow a green track on the other side, and when it runs out, carry straight on across the field to the corner opposite.

Carry straight on with a hedge concealing the Markham Brook on your left, until you are forced to turn right to a stile into the field ahead.

Over the stile, carry straight on up the hill ahead.

Follow the left hand hedge to a stile into an enclosed path, which contains nettles, brambles and a concealed hole. If it is impassable, it is easy enough to get round it.

(Note the beautiful walled garden ahead as you descend to the stile.)

When you emerge in a track, turn left between two houses. **11**

Follow the track round to the right, where there is a stile next to a gate.

Over the stile, turn left over another stile and follow the path to the right and up around a horse fence to a larger field beyond.

Follow the right hand edge of the field over the hill for about a kilometre, until you come to a footbridge in the fence ahead. **12**

Turn right along an enclosed track to a gap into the next field on the right.

Continue around the other side of a wooded gully to a kissing gate.

Turn right and follow the right hand fence past three more kissing gates around to a kissing gate next to a field gate. (It is just past an orchard and commands a view of Compton Church.)

Carry on with a fence on your left to another kissing gate and field gate into a tarmac drive, which leads down to a footbridge next to a cattle grid to emerge on the road beside Compton Dando village hall.

Turn right to find the Compton Inn opposite the church.

FROM THE COMPTON INN TO WOOLLARD

From the pub **13**, turn right and follow the road past one junction, over the bridge, past another junction and up the hill towards Keynsham.

After the last house, look for a kissing gate on the left. **14**

Go straight ahead up the hill to another kissing gate, followed by another gate.

Continue on up the hill to another kissing gate, beyond which is a mowed orchard and a mobile phone mast, so you will now be able to get a signal!

Continue across the grass to another kissing gate and steps down onto Slate Lane.

Follow the road to the right past Knowle Farm and round some bends until you find a kissing gate on your left, leading into *Wooscombe Wood*. **15**

Turn right along a clearing, which appears to be a landing strip, until you come to a wide clearing off to the left.

This appears to be a taxi way leading to a black hangar hidden among the trees.

You are looking for a footpath sign on the far side of this clearing along a wire fence, before you come to the hangar.

Follow the footpath, which can be muddy to a kissing gate onto an enclosed path, which runs above a steep gully on the left.

When you emerge through a kissing gate into a field, bear left to a small gate in a wire fence, which will be useful if they fence the gap next to it!

Follow the right hand hedge past a gateway to the bottom right hand corner of the field, where there is a kissing gate (sometimes hidden by nettles!)

Make your way through some more nettles to Smallbrook Lane. **16**

Turn right and follow the lane down hill to a road.

Turn left into Woollard.

FROM WOOLLARD TO PENSFORD

Turn left again over the road bridge across the Chew and then right towards a byway **17**.

This is where one of the most challenging stretches of the Compton Dandy Run comes out. The race is usually put on by Town and Country Harriers during August, and spectators gather here to watch the runners staggering into the road after the water has sucked the energy out of their thighs.

[You could follow the stream for about 150 m, if you don't mind getting wet legs, but you should be aware that motor vehicles are allowed to use by-ways and it would be very difficult to get out of the way of an oncoming motor bike. If you did decide to take this course, you would turn right through a kissing gate after you came out of the water and head across the field to join the main route.]

Assuming you do <u>not</u> want to get very wet, bear right across the field to a bend in the River Chew and follow the bank to a kissing gate nearby.

Go straight ahead to a track and find a kissing gate on the left.

Turn right to a stile and bridge, beyond which another kissing gate will get you back onto the track. [You might feel it was more sensible to stick to the track all the way, but that is not where the right of way goes!]

Turn left and follow the track to a bridge over the River Chew.

Over the bridge, find a kissing gate into the field ahead. Go straight on past Publow Church **18** to a kissing gate between the churchyard and the river.

Follow the path to the road and turn left across the bridge to a kissing gate on your left.

Through the gate, bear right across the field to another kissing gate and continue on the same line, past the gate near the village hall to a kissing gate onto the road in the top right hand corner.

Follow the pavement back to the Lockup, from which it is easy to find refreshment and transport.

14: COAL, STONES...
OR 'THE FOOL' -5.9 miles approx.
From the Old Lockup in Pensford -ST620637

The name of this route reflects the fact that, although Pensford has no parish church of its own, it nevertheless warrants a section all to itself in an account of the Coal Measures in 'The British Regional Geology' volume on 'The Bristol and Gloucester District'. Further information is contained in 'Colliers Way -The Somerset Coalfield' written by Peter Collier and published by Ex Libris Press in 1986, on which I have relied for much of my information. This hidden geology explains a number of things, such as the site of the magnificent Pensford Viaduct, a strange hill near Stanton Drew and the lock-up for rowdy miners, where Mr Acker Bilk starts The Pensford 10K Road Race. It also explains the wide choice of pubs in Pensford. There are three, if you include the Travellers' Rest at the top of the hill. The George and Dragon and the Rising Sun are closer to the route. Parking is a bit tight in Pensford, but it is possible to park at the village hall on the road to Publow and Compton Dando, opposite the Rising Sun, and there are a couple of spaces next to the bus stop. It is also possible

to get refreshments at the Druids Arms in Stanton Drew.
There is in any case a perfectly reasonable bus service and
the 375, 376 and 379 buses all stop at Pensford Bridge.
Because of the multiplicity of possible starting points, I have
arbitrarily begun the route description from the lockup on
the road to Woollard, which is relatively easy to find.
The sketch map has produced a large nosed skater,
whizzing along with hands behind his back. The insouciant
fellow has not a care in the world, although it is apparent
that he is about to fall flat on his back. He appears to be
taking seriously the Taoist injunction to:
  Give up sainthood, renounce wisdom.
  And it will be a hundred times better for everyone.

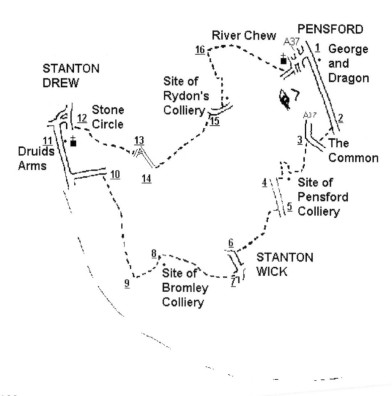

It seems a foolhardy course to me, but:
> *He who knows how to live can walk abroad*
> *Without fear of rhinoceros or tiger,*
> *He will not be wounded in battle,*
> *For in him rhinoceroses can find no place to thrust*
> *their horn*
> *Tigers no place to use their claws*
> *And weapons no place to pierce.*
> *Why is this so?*
> *Because he has no place for death to enter.*

FROM THE LOCKUP TO THE DRUID'S ARMS

From the lock-up (**1**), pass the George and Dragon as you climb towards the top of the hill. (We all have to make sacrifices sometimes!)

After the last house, look for a stile on the right beside the de-restriction sign. **2**

In the field (called The Common), follow the wire fence on the right to a stile in the corner.

Over the stile, look for another stile concealed on the left.

Over the stile, descend some steps through the trees to another stile onto the A37.

Cross the road carefully and turn right on the pavement to look for a descending road on the left. **3**

When the road bends to the right over a stream, look for a stile on the left.

Over the stile, pick your way up a rough boggy field to a stile hidden behind some brambles. (It seems to be better if you keep to the right on the way up.)

Over the stile, cross the bed of the old Bristol And Somerset Railway and follow a footpath sign to a stile a little to the left.

Over the stile, follow the path to the right, which skirts around the batch (or slag heap) of Pensford Colliery.

This path can be boggy from the water, draining out from the bottom of the slagheap, but there were cowslips growing around it when we checked it out. Peter Collier said it was overgrown when he visited, so it is probably better to visit before the nettles have grown up.

The signs to the far side of the slagheap are clear enough.

When you get to the far side, you will find that the Winding House has been converted to another use.

The way out onto the road is a gap beside the gate to the right of the building. **4**

Through the gap, turn left and follow the road until you come across a field gate on the right, just past the bus depot on the left. **5**

Over the gate, which was open when we checked, but is usually secured with barbed wire, go straight ahead to another gate over a mysterious hump.

Through this gate turn left to a new kissing gate.

This footpath runs above the line of a dismantled tramway that ran from Bromley Colliery to the railway line at Pensford Colliery. It used to run along the bottom of this field.

There are two more new kissing gates on the right, through which the path approaches a wind pump.

Past the wind pump go through another kissing gate in the corner, and head for yet another beside a new barn conversion. Go on over a stile into the road and turn left. **6**

Go straight on at a road junction and look for a stile up a drive on the right. **7**

In the field, bear right to a hedge corner and carry on to a kissing gate on the right.

Through the gate, keep going on the same line to another hedge corner and continue with the hedge on your right to another kissing gate.

Past this kissing gate, carry on to yet another hedge corner.

You cross the line of the tramway on the way. You will probably also have noticed the strange hill on the left by now. It is the batch of Bromley Colliery, which survived until 1957. According to Collier, it was still using pit ponies in 1955.

At this hedge corner, there is another kissing gate and you continue with the hedge on your left to a stile and a plank bridge. **8**

Before you get there you may notice that some badgers have been doing some mining of their own on the left. They even have their own bridge across the stream to take their old bedding into the field.

Over the plank-bridge, turn left up the hill to look for another bridge on the left into the wood that now covers the Bromley Colliery Batch.

I found a piece of coal here, which shattered in my bag on the way home, as it was too shaly. It contained the imprint of a dragonfly's wing or else an intricate leaf.

The footpath winds along parallel to the left hand hedge to a stile out of the wood.

Over the stile, carry on, up the hill with the hedge on your right and Bromley Farm straight ahead.

At the top of the field turn right through a gate (**9**) and continue with the hedge on your left until you reach a kissing gate.

Carry on, on the same line, but this time with the hedge on your right, through a series of new gates until you emerge through a kissing gate into a large field.

Your aim is the new metal gate in the far left hand corner of the field, but you may need to go through a gate on the right into a passage protected by electric fences to get there. We crawled under the fence at the bottom of the field.

Through the gate, turn right to a kissing gate into an enclosed path to the road. **10**

In the road, turn left, pass the school and then turn right at the road junction.

On your way down to the pub, you may be able to make out the stones of an inaccessible stone circle on your right, which are peeping over the hedge.

Carry on to the Druid's Arms. **11**

There are three more standing stones in the pub garden, although one of them has fallen over. For some reason they are known as the Cove.

FROM THE DRUID'S ARMS TO THE RISING SUN

Turn right at the pub, right at a crossroads and right again toward the church, which is strategically placed to protect the village from the evil influence of the standing stones.

Turn left up the concrete track into the yard of Church Farm. **12**

Follow the track to a kissing gate (You probably won't need to use it as the field gate is usually open.) and turn left.

There are more standing stones on the left. If you wanted to see them more closely, you should have taken a different route off Church Road and placed £1 in the honesty box.

There are three options ahead, a small metal gate beside a field gate, a stile and a kissing gate. You need the stile next to the kissing gate, which has some steps down on the other side.

Down the steps, bear right and head for a stile in the diagonally opposite corner of the field.

Over this stile, follow the right hand hedge to find another stile.

Go across the next field to yet another stile into a snicket between the houses.

Turn left on the pavement and turn right up 'Tarnwell'. **13**

Follow the road, to the right. It becomes a lane down to a bungalow.

At the end, turn left through a kissing gate into a field (**14**) and follow the stream on your right for about 300 metres.

Cross the stream, by a plank bridge to a kissing gate and bear left toward some trees on the horizon to another kissing gate hidden on the left on the other side of the hill.

Through the kissing gate, go straight ahead to a gated bridge over a stream.

Over the stream, follow the right hand hedge over the spur to find a stile onto a road. **15**

Turn right and then left down a bridle path. (There is a stile to the left of the gate, but the gate also opens easily.)

On the right is Old Down, which according to Peter Collier, may be the site of Rydon's or Riding's Colliery, which was worked between 1808 and 1832.

(Do not be seduced into following the path from the stile on the right, which leads into the grumpy ground left over from the days of mining. You cannot get back onto the bridle path at the bottom.)

Follow the bridle path down through two gates toward the river.

Turn right after the last gate, just before Byemills Cottage onto the Forest Path. **16**

Follow the distinct path across the field to a kissing gate, some steps and another kissing gate into another field.

Follow the even more distinct path toward the viaduct over a bridge and a kissing gate.

The Forest Path goes off to the right after the viaduct, but there is a more interesting path, which goes straight on over the river past the church to emerge at the back of the Rising Sun. This is not a right of way as far as I know, and you should only use it as a customer of the pub!

In any case, your route from here rather depends on your intentions.

If you are visiting the George and Dragon, or have left your car at the village hall, you need to cross the A37 by the pedestrian crossing and take the turning for Publow and Easter Compton.

15: CHEW MAGNA
OR THE HIPPOGRIFF 12.6 miles (approx.)
From the car park in Chew Magna -ST576631

This route begins in the car park next to the Pelican in Chew Magna (Great Chew). This should not be taken as an endorsement of the Pelican, although it does have a pleasant beer garden, because at the time of writing, the pub is up for sale. However, the major part of the car park is open to the public, and the Pelican is easier to find than the Queen's Arms, which is, arguably, the best pub in the village. The Bear and Swan also has a following, and a roaring fire in the winter season, but some feel it is more of a restaurant than the Queen's Arms, which also serves good food.

Some people, arriving in Chew Magna by one of the several buses that serve it, may content themselves with resolving once and for all the question, which is the best pub in the village, but the route offers the possibility of more extensive research.

All in all, the route must be considered as something of a macho challenge, either as an extended pub crawl, taking in the Dundry Inn, the Rising Sun and the George and

Dragon in Pensford, the Druids' Arms in Stanton Drew, the Pelican, the Bear and Swan and the Queen's Head in Chew Magna or as a run from Dundry with a sting in the tail (which is how I have usually done it). Indeed, if you are not drinking, in addition to the car park next to the Pelican, there are car parks beside Dundry Down, at the Village Hall in Pensford and beside some of the sacred stones in Stanton Drew.

One of the chief reasons for starting in Chew Magna is the fact that you get the main climb out of the way at the beginning.

The route has little that is original about it. It follows sections of the Community Forest Path, the Three Peaks Walk, the Two Rivers Way and the Samaritans' Southwest Way. On the other hand:

> *If I have a little sense*
> *I will walk in the main road.*
> *And my only fear will be straying from it.*
> *Keeping to the main road is easy.*
> *But people love to be sidetracked.*

However, this does not feel like a Taoist route. Two thirds of the route crosses the southern or "yang" slopes of the Dundry Ridge. This is a situation described by Sun Tzu in 'The Art of War' as most suitable for setting up an armed camp or for arraying troops for a battle. Even the "yin" third along the southern bank of the River Chew has a sun temple, namely the stone circles at Stanton Drew half way along it, which must surely cancel out the section's "yin" qualities.

To my eye, the sketch map resembles a hippogriff, half horse, half griffin, on the point of hauling itself to its feet like a horse before hurling itself into the air like an eagle. This reminds us of Confucius' remark about Lao Tzu -'the dragon's ascent into heaven on the winds and the clouds is something, which is beyond my knowledge. Today I have seen Lao Tzu who is perhaps like a dragon.'

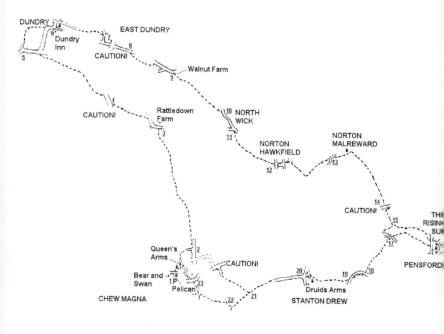

Among a number of useful buses are the 455 from Nailsea to Chew Magna and the Chew Valley Explorer from Bristol to Cheddar (672 and 674), which also visits Dundry. (Note, the 674 turns off down Chew Lane before it reaches the centre of Chew Magna.) The 683 between Keynsham and Wells and the 834 between Weston Super Mare also stop at Chew, but they only run one return journey each, so exact up to date details are unusually important.

FROM CHEW MAGNA TO THE DUNDRY INN

From the car park in Chew Magna (**1**), cross the High Street to St Andrew's Church.

Make your way through the churchyard to the village hall on the other side.

Cross the 'weak bridge' and go straight ahead up Butham Lane, past the village school.

Take the first signed footpath to the right through a yard to a kissing gate into a paddock.

Go diagonally left through the paddock to a stone stile.

Turn right up the lane, and then turn left at a road junction.

Take the first footpath on the left up some steps into a farmyard. **2**

Go straight across the farmyard to a stile into a field.

In the field, follow the stream on the left, which is hidden by a hedge, past a gate on the left and an isolated tree to find a gate in the fence ahead.

Through the gate bear left up the hill in front to a ladder-stile in the hedge on the horizon.

Over the stile –the footpath goes just left of straight on across a cornfield to a hedge corner in the direction of Rattledown Farm (the white house on the horizon!)

The farmer is supposed to keep the path clear, but I am yet to see this happen here. So, if the path is thigh high in wheat or some other crop, you may prefer to follow the hedge left around field after the ladder stile until you reach the stile in the second field corner.

If you have managed to follow the footpath across the field, follow the track left (keeping a hedge on your right) to find the stile in the corner of the field.

Over this stile keep the hedge on your right until you come across a stile in a hedge ahead of you.

Over this stile, keep the hedge on your left to a stile at the bottom of the hill. Last time I checked the stile was overgrown with nettles, but luckily there was a gap to the right.

Go diagonally left up the hill to a hedge corner.

Keep the hedge on your left as you climb up to a double stile over a bridge on the left. Take care with the first stile. The rail is damaged.

Over the stile, turn right and keep on up hill with the hedge on your right until you see a stile ahead onto the road beside a barn conversion next to Rattledown Farm called Homefields. **3**

Over the stile turn left up the road and around the corner to look for a stile on the left.

Over this stile go diagonally right to a field gate.

Keep to the right hand hedge over two stiles. Then keep going to a gate onto the main road. CAUTION! **4**

Cross the road carefully, turn right past two houses ('Highlands' and 'Crown Hill') and look for a stile on the left.

Over the stile, keep to the right hand hedge through a gateway and past a manure heap to a stile in the corner.

Over the stile, make for a garden gate to the left of a radio mast. Follow the path alongside a chain-link fence onto a metalled track.

Climb the stile on the left and turn left along the left hand hedge, through a gateway to a stile (really a gate wired shut) into a field.

Go straight ahead with a hedge on your right to a gate.

Through the gate follow the track to a road.

You have probably noticed a potential shortcut along the road to the pub. However, if you take this less scenic route, you will miss the splendid view of the Clifton Suspension Bridge and the Severn Bridges from Dundry Down.

Turn left and then first right to find a kissing gate beside a field gate onto Dundry Down. **5**

Keep to the track along the left hand edge until it swings to the right.

Leave the track and follow the footpath signs along the hedge side until you see a kissing gate onto the second part of the Down.

Through the gate, bear right towards Dundry Church and a field gate beside a car park.

Keep going along the road toward the church and the Dundry Inn. **6**

The tower of the Church of St Michael is visible for miles around. The tower is presently open on the first Saturday of the month and affords spectacular views of Bristol and the surrounding countryside. Some people will be more interested in the pub next to the church.

FROM THE DUNDRY INN TO PENSFORD

From the pub, turn left and then right again around the church.

Turn right again along a lane that follows the top of the escarpment to a gate.

There is actually a stile to the right of this gate, but I missed it for years because it was hidden by nettles.

Continue straight ahead to a stile beside another gate into a field.

Keep the hedge on your left until you find a stile in the corner.

Over this stile, follow a track lined with stones until you find a gate on the right.

Go through the gate and turn left to another gate onto a metalled road. 7

This is not the course that the footpath takes on the map, but it is the only viable route.

On the road turn right and go up to West Dundry Lane.

At the junction turn left, and proceed to the main road. CAUTION!

Cross the main road and go straight on to find a stile on the right into a field. **8**

Over the stile bear left to another stile.

Over this stile, keep on, along the top of a steep slope to find a stone stile ahead onto a road. (It is a bit overgrown).

On the road, turn right and go down the hill until the second turning on the right.

At this junction, go straight on through some gates onto the metalled drive to Walnut Farm Cottage. **9**

Bear right in front of a barn to find a stile at the end of a Leyland Cypress hedge.

Over this stile and another one, go straight on down the hill and through a gate in a wire fence.

Through the gateway, keep the fence on your left until you reach another gate.

Go straight on through this gate and then bear slightly right down hill to find a stile in the hedge ahead.

Go straight ahead to a stile onto a minor road. **10**

Turn right and descend to a junction.

Turn right again and immediately look for a stile into the field on your left. **11**

Go straight ahead across the field to another stile.

Over this stile follow the well-used path to an unnecessarily substantial double stile and bridge over a rivulet.

Bear left to another double stile thirty metres further on.

Go straight ahead to another stile and turn left to find another double stile in front of you.

Go straight ahead across the next field to find a substantial footbridge over an unnamed stream.

 Keep going through the scrub to find a stile into the field on the left

Over this stile, bear right to find a stile into a road in Norton Hawkfield. **12**

I have never seen a hawk here, but I have seen a raven,
which also flies over the fields to the north of Chew Magna.
In the road, turn right and then first left.

At a junction turn left then right into a farmyard.

Go straight on through the farmyard and turn right onto a farm track.

Go through two gates to follow the edge of a mini-escarpment around a wire fence.

Go through a kissing gate and continue to the right hand corner of the field and a kissing gate onto the road.
On the road, turn left and look for a kissing gate on the right.
13

Through the gate, head up the diagonal path to one kissing gate in the middle of a wire fence and another in the opposite corner of the field.

Through the gate, bear right through another kissing gate into a field (unless the field gate is open.)

In this field, follow the track up the hill, over a grass landing strip and straight on up. (Take care! This is an active landing strip!)

At the end of the field, there is a gap into an enclosed, rocky lane, which descends to the B3130. **CAUTION!** **14**

On the road, turn left to find a kissing into the field on the right.

In the field turn right (back the way you have just come) to find another kissing gate next to a gate.

Next, turn left and follow the fence down hill to another kissing gate. **15**

SHORTCUT

If you do not want to stop for a drink in Pensford -you might be running for example -bear right to a kissing gate into a field that often contains donkeys.

Go through the field to a kissing gate onto a track.

Turn left and cross the River Chew.

Turn right over a kissing gate to rejoin the main route at **17.**

In the next field, bear left to find another kissing gate next to the river.

Follow the river downstream through two more kissing gates, the second of which takes you into a conservation woodland. Keep going along the track to the right, through another kissing gate under the viaduct and down the track which turns into a tarmac road to emerge next to The Rising Sun in Pensford. **16**

FROM PENSFORD TO STANTON DREW

From the Rising Sun, turn right across the Old Bridge over the River Chew and turn right at the junction and then right again to find a gap by a gate into a car park with a kissing gate out the other side. Follow the footpath under the viaduct. **(NB If you are going for the pub crawl option, don't forget the George and Dragon on the other side of the main road!)**

Go through another kissing gate and follow the path over a wooden bridge and alongside a path usually bounded by an electric fence to another kissing gate.

Follow the clear path across a field often occupied by reasonably placid horses to another kissing gate.

Through the gate, go down some steps and through another kissing gate on the right into a field.

In the field, turn left to find a kissing gate to the left of Byemills Cottage.

Pass the cottage to another kissing gate on the opposite side of a bridle path. **17**

In the field, go straight ahead keeping the River Chew on your right.

After a bridge with a stile at each end, the path bears left uphill away from the river to a mini gate beside a muddy gateway.

Through the gate, turn right and continue with the hedge on your right to a kissing gate onto a lane. **18**

Cross the road through a wicket gate in a galvanised steel field gate into the field opposite and bear right keeping the lane on your right until you rejoin the road through a similar gate. **19**

Cross the road through a third wicket gate and follow a track into a market garden.

At the end of the track, bear right around the bottom edge of the field and around to a kissing gate about fifty yards up from far corner of field.

Through the gate, go straight ahead to find another kissing gate in the corner of the field.

Next, bear right to a gate next to a metalled track. (Watch out for electric fences, which are used to manage dairy cattle.)

Follow the farm track past the stone circles on the right and through a farmyard. There is a kissing gate here too, but the farm gate is usually open. (There is usually an electric fence or at least a piece of string across the track here too.) Turn right when you reach the road.

Take the first left past some cottages to a crossroads. **20**

The Druid's Arms is up to the left, if you are on a social ramble, otherwise you will need to go straight on.

FROM STANTON DREW TO CHEW MAGNA

Take Sandy Lane (metalled at this point.)
Follow the lane past the last house, where it becomes a well-maintained farm track. **21**

RUNNERS' SHORTCUT

If you have started from Dundry, you may prefer to avoid the pleasures of Chew Magna on this occasion. In which case, look out for a kissing gate on the right and descend through the fields to a bridge over the River Chew.

Continue up a metalled lane to the B3130.

Turn left and then right up a bridle path, which goes uphill and then bends to the right to emerge at a crossroads.

Turn right and look for some steps up to a farmyard on the left to rejoin the main route. **2**

Otherwise: keep on the track until it turns to the right. Keep on the track ignoring a stile beside a farm gate, until you can turn left over a footbridge and stile. **22**

Ascend a well-trodden path diagonally right through the field to an open gate. Descend on the same line to the bottom corner of the field.

Take care on the steep and sometimes slippery descent into a sunken lane and turn right to find some stiles and a bridge over the River Chew.

Over the bridge take the path through the field to a stile onto the main road. **23**

Cross the road carefully to a stone stile between some ornamental gates and a cricket pitch. Follow the drive to Chew Court.

Turn right before the gates and follow the lane around the walls until St Andrew's Church comes into view.

Go over the stone stile into the churchyard and follow the path to the left, back to the High Street (unless you want to visit the Queen's Arms on the right).

The Queen's Arms

The Bear and Swan

The car park is over the road, next to the Pelican.

16: A BIRD IN THE HAND
OR PLOP, 'THE OWL WHO WAS AFRAID OF THE DARK' -about 6.4 miles
From the Bird in the Hand in Long Ashton -ST540702

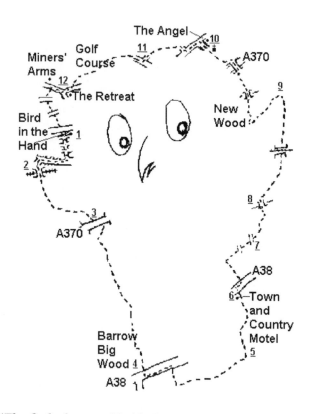

'The Owl who was Afraid of the Dark' by Jill Tomlinson is not the sort of book you need to read to know what it is about. Everything you need to know is in the title, except for the fact that Plop overcame his fear, which you could have guessed, because it is a children's book after all.

The Tao Te Ching is a different sort of book, which is evident from the fact that it starts:

The Tao that can be told is not the eternal Tao.
The name that can be named is not the eternal name.
It goes on:
The nameless is the beginning of heaven and earth.
The named is the mother of 10 000 things.
Ever desireless, one can see the mystery.
Ever desiring, one can see the manifestations.
These two spring from the same source,
But differ in name.

It is an accident that this route is named after the Bird in the Hand. It could have started from the Miners' Arms, or the Angel, or the Retreat or even the Town and Country Motel -in which case it is probable that Plop, the owl, would never have appeared. He could have ended up as kobold or a knocker from a mine, or a bullock from the field next to the motel, or a cute angel, or Robin Hood from the Retreat (formerly Robin Hood's Retreat).

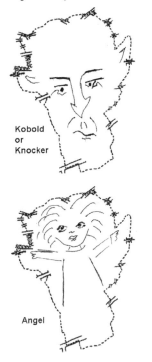

Kobold
or
Knocker

Angel

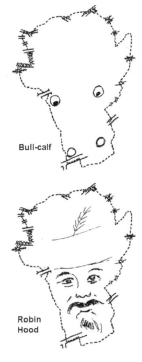

Bull-calf

Robin
Hood

Or maybe not!

Plop is not much of a name. It fact it might be termed a non-name. And it is instructive that he overcame his fear of the dark by attaching names to it: exciting; kind; fun; necessary; fascinating; wonderful and beautiful. Only you can say whether this route would be more enjoyable, if it had another name.

However, we can be sure that no other name than Plop - 'The Owl who was afraid of the Dark' could have taken us back to the beginning of the Tao Te Ching.

> *This appears as darkness.*
> *Darkness within darkness*
> *The gate of all mystery.*

Well might this darkness confuse the brain of an owl -it certainly makes me think I could do with a drink! That was apparently the preferred route to mystical enlightenment for Alan Watts, the renowned writer and lecturer on eastern religion who died in 1973.[1] However, as we shall see, it is wise to remember the Wurzels!

Parking is a problem at all the Long Ashton pubs, so it may be better to park in Keedwell Lane for the Bird in the Hand, or else use public transport, particularly in view of the alcoholic temptations along the route. Long Ashton is served by the 350, 351 and 353 services between Bristol and Weston Super Mare, the 354 from Bristol to Nailsea and the 355, 362, 363 and 364 to Clevedon.

1 NB: Solent (adj.) - Descriptive of the state of serene self-knowledge reached through drink (in The Meaning of Liff by Douglas Adams and John Lloyd - 1983).

FROM THE BIRD IN THE HAND TO BARROW COMMON

With your back to the pub **1**, turn left and left again down Yeo Lane.

Go as straight as possible down Yeomeads and Elmhurst Gardens until you can go no further.

Turn right at a T-junction.

Proceed down Penshurst Gardens until you reach a cul-se-sac (Paulman Gardens) on the left.

Here the route joins the Monarch's Way, a long distance footpath following the route of the flight of Charles II from the final battle of the Civil War at Worcester via Abbot's Leigh near Bristol to the south coast and France.

Go down the footpath at end of the cul-de-sac.

Over a stile turn left. **2**

Cross the railway-bridge and go straight on past a barn up the hill to a stile.

Over the stile, go diagonally left up the field to another stile.

Keep left round the field to another stile.

Go down the first set of steps; then follow the wire fence on the right as the steps descend to the left. **3**

At the bottom, bear left across the bare earth under the dual carriageway to find a track between the brambles.

Pass the plank walk (unless it is really muddy). Avoid the track up to the right and keep straight on to a stile.

The track leads off in the direction of the former mental hospital at Barrow Gurney, but it does not seem to get there. The hospital, which was sold for development in 2005, was made famous by the Wurzels in 'Drink up thy Zider' a song, which suggested that it was the ultimate destination of all Zider drinkers. This may serve as a warning to those, such as myself, who know that there is some excellent scrumpy behind the bar at the Bird in the Hand, and also at the Miners in Providence Lane. (Actually, they often have it at the Angel as well, and there is some good bottled stuff at the Retreat!)

Over this stile, follow the path to a stile into a field.

Over to the right you can just make out Ridings Wood, part of the Wild Country, which used to make up the grounds of the hospital.

In the field, turn right and follow the line of a hedge to a stile into a tree-tunnel track.

Over a stile into the field at the far end follow the left hedge to a stile into a tiny copse. (The going is better away from the hedge.)

Go through the copse to a stile and head for Barrow Big Wood ahead. (You need to bear left through a gate into a second field, turn right and then bear left up a bank to find a stile into the wood ahead.)

Go straight on through the wood to find a double stile next to the reservoir.

Go straight on, on a crushed stone path to find a snicket between the houses onto the A38. **4**

Cross the main road carefully; then turn left along the pavement to find a footpath on the right past a petrol station (the footpath sign is on the left of the road).

Follow the track past some stables and up the hill to find a stile into the field on the left.

Here the route leaves the Monarch's Way to join the Community Forest Path.

FROM BARROW COMMON TO THE ANGEL

Over the stile, go straight across a grass field to find a pair of gates into the field opposite. There is a stile to the right of the right hand gate, but it has become overgrown with brambles, so most people climb the gate. Over the stile (or the right hand gate *(NB Always climb a gate at the hinge end.)*) follow the left hedge to a stile.

Over the stile follow an enclosed path to a double stile over a stream.

Go up the bank between some brambles then bear right up a long field, usually stocked with horses, to find a leaning gate towards the middle of the top hedge. **5**

Over the gate, turn left to find a gap in the hedge.

Through the gap, bear left to a stile in the corner of the field. *The last time I used this route, there were some additional temporary stiles built in the fences on either side of a pipeline.* In any case, bear right down the hill to find a stile beside a gate onto a track down to the A38, which emerges next to the Town and Country Motel. **6**

Over the main road go right to find a stile.

Over this stile, go straight across the field to another stile.

Over this stile, bear right to find a stile along the hedge on your right.

This is the point at which the ring road extension to the A38 is planned to pass.

Over this stile, follow the hedge on your right to a pair of stiles over a farm track, then carry on down-slope in the same direction to another pair of stiles over the access road to the landfill site. **7**

Bear left to a stile in a wire fence and carry on, on same line, to another stile in a hedge.

Over this stile, turn sharp left down the hedge side and over another stile into a thicket.

Track right through the thicket to find a stile out into a field.

Track left around the brambles to find a path to a double stile and bridge over Colliter's Brook. **8**

Turn right in between the stream and the landfill site (ignoring a second bridge on your right) to find a tunnel under the main line to Exeter and beyond.

In the open follow the right hand edge of the field past factories and deep water until the path goes through a gap in the hedge ahead.

Do not go through the gap. 9

Instead, turn left along side of field, keeping a hedge on your right.

The stretch along the valley bottom is under threat from the central government demand for more housing in this area. I suppose they could point to the nearby tip and say, 'It's not really countryside. Where's your problem!'

Pass one gateway; then go through the next gateway on your right, labelled with a footpath sign.

Through the gate turn sharp right alongside a strip of woodland, to find a leaning gate on your right. (There is a footpath sign on the left of the track -the gateway is obscured by a low branch.)

Over the gate, bear right to find a substantial bridge over a ditch or rhine.

Over the bridge carry straight on along a filthy, muddy track reinforced by rubble to find a cattle bridge over the A370.

Keep on the track through the cow dung until you reach a galvanised gate on your right, which leads up through the field beside the graveyard to a kissing gate.

In the graveyard, turn left to find the gate out of the graveyard into a road.

Go straight on up the road to emerge next to the Angel Inn. **10**

FROM THE ANGEL TO THE BIRD IN THE HAND

Cross over the main road and turn left along the pavement, until you can turn right up Hobwell Lane.

At the top of the lane, climb a stile and go diagonally left up the field to a stile hidden in the top left hand corner. Over this stile, continue up and left around the top of a private garden with views across the valley onto a drive.

On the drive turn left down the hill and then right up past Folleigh Close. **11**

Take the footpath onto the Golf Course.

Keep left on a footpath alongside the left hand fence. The path is narrow and rough. There is just one false trail off to the left before a turning to a metal kissing gate onto a road.

Turn right to a T-junction beside the Retreat (formerly the Robin Hood's Retreat). **12**

Turn right up the hill towards the Miner's Rest.

Find a footpath descending on your left, just before the pub. Follow the path across two roads (It becomes Brocks Lane.) to emerge opposite the Bird in the Hand.

17: THE GREEN ANGEL
OR 'THE MESSENGER' -about 7.5 miles
From the Angel in Long Ashton -ST552710

This classic route begins from the Angel in Long Ashton, whose double sided inn-sign reveals something of the ambiguity of the idea of an angel. The word originates from a Greek word meaning a messenger. As a notice in the pub informs us the inn's name was originally the Angel's Salutation, which links it with the archangel Gabriel's greeting to the Virgin Mary. (I.E. Hail Mary etc.) But the inn-sign on the outside of the pub reminds us that there are other angels. The angel in white could be intended to refer to Gabriel, but who is the dark angel, dressed in black and sitting by the light of the moon?

There are traditions of many messengers from god apart from Gabriel. The angel with the fiery sword who was charged the task of driving Adam and Eve springs to mind, and there is St Michael, the leader of the heavenly host, who defeats Satan in the last days. And we should not forget that Satan himself is a fallen angel in Milton's Paradise Lost.

The route map has produced another ambiguous figure, which appears to represent a helmeted female soldier, either an Amazon or another kind of messenger. It is written in the Tao Te Ching:

> *A good soldier is not violent.*
> *A good fighter is not angry.*
> *A good winner is not vengeful.*
> *This is known as the virtue of not striving.*
> *This is known as the ability to deal with people.*
> *This, since ancient time, has been known as*
> *   the ultimate unity with heaven.*

This image of soldiering is totally at odds the macho image portrayed in many war films, but is entirely appropriate as a description of this soldier, who appears to be a woman.

Another ambiguous image, connected with this route is the sculptured head of the Green Man, which was chosen by designer, Sally Mundy, for the cover of the first Crossing Boundaries book. (I had to hurriedly create a new route (the Dragon), because I had not written a suitable one that passed the sculpture.) Since then, I have had the image in the forefront of my mind. It seems to me to represent the ultimate dependency of man on his environment. This is symbolised by the foliage creeping up out of the ground to envelop his face, but also by the map of the countryside, laid out on the flat of his head. Instead of a brain, he has a representation of the landscape he faces.

The Green Man also changes the significance of the George, especially when taken alongside the Angel, because the connection turns him into Green George. Green George is a manifestation of Al Khidr or the Green One, a mysterious Islamic figure, an immortal alongside Idris (Enoch), Ilyas(Elias) and Isa (Jesus). He was the companion of Moses in the Koran and is regarded as a protector of travellers. He is also an embodiment of the spring. He is regarded as equivalent to the Christian St George, especially in Syria. He is nowhere regarded as female, but he is regarded as an angel by many, and angels have no gender at all. In this context, Al Khidr stands for the mystical, universalist strand of Islam.

What then is the message?

The key is the location of the mutilated image of the Green Man in the deer park, a piece of nature, similarly truncated and isolated. He glances up to the right, in the direction of the extended quarry in the far corner of the Ashton Court Estate. In front of his face, the Community Forest Path heads off towards the tower of Dundry Church on the horizon, crossing the A370 and the A38, between which is a landfill site, a building site proposed by the then Deputy Prime Minister, John Prescott, and the route of an extension to the Bristol ring road, planned by the Southwest Regional quango.

Refreshments, including non-alcoholic refreshments are available at the Angel and the George.

Long Ashton is served by the 350, 351 and 353 services between Bristol and Weston Super Mare, the 354 from Bristol to Nailsea and the 355, 362, 363 and 364 to Clevedon.

FROM THE ANGEL TO THE GREEN MAN

If the gates to Ashton Court are open, simply turn right at the front door of the Angel **1** and go along the pavement to the Lodge Gate. (Take care crossing the Road.)

Through the Lodge Gate, follow the drive.

Before Ashton Court Mansion comes into view, turn right along the track through a little wood, which conceals a grotto or icehouse. Go through an iron-gate and follow the gravel path to some steps. Up the steps, go straight on to the corner and through some trees to emerge by the back entrance to the mansion. * **2**

If, like me, you are in the habit of running at night, you may find that the Lodge Gates are shut. In that case, turn right towards Bristol, and follow the wall to the Dovecote public house.

Turn left down a footpath at the far side of the pub.

Continue along the path until you reach a playing field.

In the field, follow the left hand fence until you reach a wooden stile on the left into a linear wood.

Go over this stile and another into the park.

In the park, make your way towards the mansion, and turn right, keeping the ha-ha on your left until you reach a kissing gate, which brings you to the back entrance of the mansion ***2**.

Follow the Forest Path sign, which indicates the route over the drive to a pair of silver birch trees. Continue, on same line, to the corner of a wood, where there is a forestry road alongside a deer fence. Turn left up the road to a kissing gate into the deer park.

When the track bends to the left, look for a path through the deer park (marked by white posts) that goes in and out of a dip and continues to the corner of another wood.

At the wood corner, follow a track, which keeps the wood on the left and a sculpture of the Green Man on your right. **3**

FROM THE GREEN MAN TO THE GEORGE

Continue up the hill, through a kissing gate and past the Lodge Gate onto the mountain cycle path through the trees opposite.

Keep to the cycle path until you find a gap beside a pair of iron gates in the wall on the right (past the miniature railway). **4**

From the gap, turn left along Abbots Leigh Road towards some traffic lights. Just before the lights, cross the main road into Valley Road. Go up Valley Road then follow the cycle path to the left of the cottages in the wood. Go through a hole in the wall and follow the cycle path through the wood to a metalled drive. **5**

In the drive, turn right and follow the cycle path through the woods, past the car parks and a cottage.

When the cycle path veers off to the right downhill towards the river, keep going straight on (or slightly to the left) until the track joins another drive beyond another parking place. **6**

Turn left and continue along the drive to a major road. **7**

Turn left and cross the road from the lay-by opposite Sandy Lane.

If you do not want to stop at the George, go down Sandy Lane to find a path on the left after about 600m. Turn left again in the track to rejoin the main route at the Abbot's Pool. **8**

Otherwise: turn left and follow the pavement up to The George.

The George at Abbot's Leigh

FROM THE GEORGE TO THE ANGEL

From the pub, turn right down Manor Road.

Look for a footpath off to the right, which cuts off the corner to Manor Lane and continue across it down a lane.

At the end, there is footpath down to the Abbot's Pool.

Follow the path down some steps then up the other side to a junction. **8**

Turn left and follow the track past the Abbot's Pool and through a car park to a road.

Cross the road and continue up the hill and past fifty acre wood on a track that emerges in a metalled road.

Keep going straight ahead to Beggar Bush Lane.

Cross the road **(Be careful, it is a bit of a rat-run.)** Turn left and then right through the hole in the wall into the Ashton Court Estate. **9**

Through the Hole in the Wall, turn right.

The cycle path through the trees is currently out of bounds for a combination of conservation and safety reasons.

Continue parallel to the wall and Beggar Bush Lane until you reach a hedge and some trees at the end of the estate.

Turn left and continue to a gravelled track.

Turn left and immediately right down the side of a wood.

At the bottom of the track, turn right on the track along the top edge of the deer park.

Take the second track on your left down towards Clarken Coombe.

At the bottom of the track, look for a keyhole stile to the right. **10**

Cross the road (carefully) to a stile and gate into a golf course.

Take a path that goes straight ahead uphill and across two fairways and then descends through some rough ground to a kissing gate into an enclosed path.

Follow this path into a road and then follow the footpath sign up the first road to the left.

Follow the path down a drive and then a footpath on to the right, avoiding gated drives. **11**

Follow the path alongside a garden and down over a stile.

In the field, follow the path to a stile and gate in the diagonally opposite corner.

Follow the drive down to the road, and then turn left to return to the Angel.